ESTATE PLANNING SIMPLIFIED

ESTATE PLANNING SIMPLIFIED

YOUR FAMILY
YOUR PLAN
YOUR LEGACY

NICOLE D'AMBROGI, ESQ., LL.M.

Opening Remarks

If you are reading this, chances are that the thought of leaving this world without a plan has crossed your mind. Who can blame you?

Truthfully, nothing is more important than the safety and security of your family. That is why estate planning is essential. Unfortunately, a lot of people leave this planning to the last minute, or worse, never get to it at all.

You made the right choice by picking up this book. That means you have taken that all-important step toward securing the future for you and your family. You are in good company because you are joining the hundreds of people, I have guided through this topic in my law practice.

Estate planning is my specialty. It is what I am known for. I have been consistently ranked as one of the leading attorneys in estate planning, not just in the State of California, but nationally.

When I completed my service in the US Navy, I wanted to continue making a difference in other people's lives. To me, family is everything. I started my own legal practice because I wanted to continue to serve in an impactful way. I am glad I did. I have changed the lives of so many people and continue to do so today.

I have written this book for you, so you can plan to protect and provide for the most important asset in your life, your family. This book is intended to be a primer to your estate planning journey. I recommend reading this book before meeting with a qualified estate planning attorney so that you have a foundation to build from.

So, please read on and do not hesitate to contact me if you would like to discuss planning for your family's future. I am only a phone call or email away.

Sincerely
Nicole D'Ambrogi, Esq., LL.M.
Principal
(619) 550-3080
San Diego Legacy Law, PC
www.SDLegacyLaw.com

CONTENTS

FOREWORD

By Jonathan A Mintz, Esq.
Partner, Evergreen Legacy Planning, LLP

It is my genuine pleasure to introduce you to this book, Estate Planning Simplified, by my friend and colleague, Nicole D'Ambrogi. I've had the pleasure of collaborating with Nicole on several client matters, and I can say firsthand that Nicole is a professional dedicated to helping Americans create estate plans that work. Understanding estate planning is a critical first step in this process.

As an estate planning attorney myself, I know estate planning can be a complex topic, and some professionals seem to make it complex for complexity's sake. But as the title suggests, in Estate Planning Simplified, Nicole has distilled estate planning to its core and simplified even the most complex topics.

Understanding estate planning concepts is critical in my opinion because all Americans need at least some type of proactive plan. There is often the misperception that estate planning is only for the wealthy, and "… if I'm not wealthy (by some subjective standard) I don't need an estate plan." This belief is often combined with a second common misperception that estate planning is "planning for one's death," and who wants to plan for their own death?

In my experience these two common misperceptions couldn't be further from the truth – and they frequently discourage proactive estate planning. Why does every adult need some type of estate plan? Quite simply, everyone I know would prefer to have a say in how they should be cared for if they become disabled – and they would also like to decide what should happen to their stuff when they pass. In fact, as to the latter, your state has a "default" plan for you if you die without your own plan. That default plan is called dying intestate, or intestacy, and with intestacy your state legislature decides who receives what percentage of your property and how. Further, since minors (and some disabled persons) cannot own property in any U.S. jurisdiction, if a minor receives any portion of your property under your state's intestacy laws, the court remains actively involved in overseeing that property – obviously, at a cost. And once the minor attains majority, he or she receives 100% of the inheritance outright! Neither of these are ideal in my experience.

Most Americans would rather decide themselves who should receive their assets, and how those assets should be distributed. Chapters 2 and 3 discuss these important topics in detail.

In Chapter 4, Nicole discusses the critical subject of incapacity planning; approximately one in four Americans live with some form of disability, and the majority of Americans will be disabled, even if only temporarily, at some point during their lifetime. Thus, incapacity planning is absolutely essential and often overlooked.

Chapter 5 addresses Wills in detail and how to create an effective and enforceable Will. A surprise to many, like intestacy, one's use of a Will dictates that their assets will go through probate. Probate is simply a public court process by which beneficiaries are ascertained and assets are retitled from the name of a decedent to his or her beneficiaries.

In Chapter 6, Nicole addresses the critical subject of Revocable Trusts, which in my opinion are the foundation of any successful estate plan for numerous reasons, including probate avoidance. Chapter 7 includes additional ways to avoid probate through titling and beneficiary designations.

Finally, Chapters 8 and 9 explore the more advanced topics of Retirement Planning and Taxes, including strategies to minimize tax. Even these more advanced topics are addressed in a straightforward and relatively simple way.

So ... Congratulations! You've taken an important first step in learning about estate planning for you and your loved ones. Best of luck with your planning.

Jonathan A. Mintz, Esq.
Partner, Evergreen Legacy Planning, LLP

CHAPTER 1
ABOUT ESTATE PLANNING

Planning is bringing the future into the present so you can do something about it now.

— Alan Lakein

P ut simply, estate planning is the process through which an individual, or a family, plans for the transfer of assets in anticipation of disability and death.

Assets can include real property, investments, cars, jewelry, cash, personal property, and even that rare stamp collection. Basically, the individual can decide to pass on whatever he or she deems of value to their beneficiaries (i.e., the recipients of the inheritance).

The purpose of an estate plan is to retain as much of the individual's wealth as possible and to maximize the benefits flowing onto beneficiaries. By maximizing wealth, I am not just referring to the income a beneficiary receives.

Estate planning typically achieves the following objectives:
- Ensuring most of the estate (comprised of assets) is transferred to the beneficiaries, in an orderly and structured manner.
- To pay the least amount of state and/or federal taxes upon transfer of the estate.
- Where required, nominating guardians of children considered minors (i.e., children under the age of 18 or 21, depending on state law).
- Shielding your beneficiaries from the lengthy and costly probate court process.

What does an Estate plan consist of?

Your estate plan is comprised of a collection of legal documents. These documents cover the who, what, where, when, and how your assets will be transferred after your passing; and what happens when you can no longer look after yourself or your estate should you become incapacitated.

Unfortunately, disability and incapacity can strike any family at any time. A tragic accident can shift the focus of a family within a matter of seconds. Planning for your ultimate demise is hard enough, but if you add the thought of having to plan for your long-term disability or incapacity makes the conversation even harder.

According to the U.S. Centers for Disease Control and Prevention (CDC)[1], 61 million adults in the United States live with a disability. This is approximately one in four adults in the U.S. The good news is not every disability will leave you incapable of managing your affairs, but the question we must ask ourselves is: what if it does?

Your estate plan needs to cover both scenarios, and sooner rather than later. A well drafted estate plan will consist of:

- Will (commonly referred to as: Last Will and Testament),
- Revocable Living Trust,
- Durable Power of Attorney,
- Advance Healthcare Directive, and
- Living Will

---

[1] CDC (2019). Disability Impacts All of Us.

Will (Last Will and Testament)

A will is a legally binding document outlining how the testator (the person writing the will) intends to distribute their assets after death. The will also names an executor (the representative of the deceased), the guardians of any minor children, and includes directions about how any taxes and/or debts will be paid.

The Will is used as a map for the probate court to follow. If there is no Will the court will default to the state's plan regarding the disposition of your assets and beneficiaries.

Revocable Living Trust

A trust is a legal entity set up to hold, preserve, and distribute all your assets. This is one of the best vehicles available to avoid probate and protect your assets.

I like to explain to my clients that the revocable living trust is like a giant purse. Like a purse, a trust is created to hold all our valuable assets. During our life, we control the assets in the trust similar to the way we would control the contents of the purse. We generally do not need someone else's permission to take things out of our purse, and if you own the trust like you own the purse, you do not need someone else's permission to take things out of the trust. The benefit of having your assets in a revocable living trust is that you can easily hand off the management of the assets to someone else, either during your incapacity or upon your death. Any asset held in the trust will avoid the probate process.

Durable Power of Attorney

The Durable Power of Attorney enables someone else to step into your shoes and manage your finances if you are incapacitated or unable to make your own financial decisions. This can be a very broad power, or you may restrict the powers of your agent. Selecting your Durable Power of Attorney should be done carefully.

Advanced Healthcare Directive

The Advanced Healthcare Directive (also a Healthcare Power of Attorney) is a document that appoints an agent to make medical decisions on your behalf in the event you are incapacitated and are unable to make those decisions for yourself. Within the Advanced Healthcare Directive, you will state your intent for organ and tissue donation, what happens to your body (buried, cremated, donated), pain and discomfort, and other medical decisions that are personal in nature.

Living Will

A Living Will is often confused with the Last Will and Testament (discussed above), however, a Living Will pertains to your medical intent in the event you are in a terminal and irreversible condition and are unable to communicate your wishes regarding life sustaining treatment.

Health Information Privacy Authorization Act (HIPAA) Waiver

Known generally as a HIPAA waiver, the Health Information Privacy Authorization Act waiver authorizes your healthcare providers to inform and discuss your personal health status, treatments, diagnosis, and any other information related to your medical care with the person(s) you designate. This document does not authorize someone to make decisions on your behalf.

Assessing Your Personal Situation

Your estate plan should be assessed regularly as your personal situation changes. Time never stands still, so why should you and your approach to estate planning?

My suggestion is to reassess your estate plan after important changes in your life, such as getting married, having children, buying a house, getting private health insurance coverage, retiring, and so on.

When you reach a milestone, ask yourself whether your estate plan is still problem-proof. If the answer is "no," "I don't know," or "maybe," then a conversation with your attorney is worth having.

You and your family will benefit in the long run by taking a proactive approach to estate planning that evolves as your personal circumstances do.

Think of your estate plan as needing periodic check-ups, much like physical exams with your doctor. Although everything may seem like it is great on the outside, having a second set of eyes on the situation is sometimes very helpful. Your family dynamics may not have changed, but that does not mean the law has not. I recommend seeing your estate planning attorney once every 3 years.

Your Estate

Your "estate" is comprised of everything you own that has some form of value (especially monetary value). It should include any real property (i.e., land and improvements or buildings), business interests or shareholdings, bank accounts, cash, automobiles, boats, jewelry, and any other personal holdings that you ascribe some value.

Think long and hard about what you want to include in your estate plan and ensure you cover everything. It is important to determine who will get what, but it also protects your loved ones from hefty tax bills and an unpleasant probate process.

Who Are Your Beneficiaries?

Your beneficiaries are individuals or groups to which you would like to pass your estate. They often include your spouse, children, siblings, close friends, or organizations. You decide who inherits your assets and in what amounts.

There are two types of beneficiaries: primary beneficiaries and contingent beneficiaries.

- Primary beneficiaries are your primary choice to inherit the estate. When the testator's death occurs, these beneficiaries are first to claim the assets.
- Contingent beneficiaries are the back-up beneficiaries who inherit the estate if there is no living primary beneficiary.

If you are going to leave part of your estate to children who are under the legal age of majority (18 or 21, depending on the state), these beneficiaries will be categorized as minors.

Minors cannot legally own property until they reach the age of majority (i.e., 18 or 21) or an age designated within the documents, if older than the age of majority.

You decide who inherits your
assets and in what amounts.

Beneficiaries are discussed at length in Chapter 2 of this book.

Providing for Young Children

It is common to leave part or all your estate to your children. If your children are above the legal age (i.e., 18 or 21), they can legally inherit the estate without delay due to age after you die.

However, if your children are minors under your state's law (states vary in the age of majority they declare), the estate will be controlled by a court-supervised guardian, a conservator, or it may be placed in a restricted account as ordered by a judge and state law.

Court-supervised Guardian or Conservator

This person is appointed by a court to manage a minor's legal and financial affairs, and/or personal care. Often a guardian/conservator will be appointed in the event the minor's parents have died or become incapacitated.

Conservator

This individual manages the estate (assets of the minor) on behalf of a minor and can be appointed by the executor of the estate. This individual is also referred to as a guardian in some states.

The role of a conservator is an important one; they effectively manage all the finances of the minor and make payments on their behalf. The conservator manages payments for expenses such as healthcare, education, and maintenance (e.g., clothing), so their appointment should be considered carefully.

If the minor inherits real property, it is the conservator who will pay for the property's expenses, including loan repayments, insurance, repairs, and other upkeep.

Restricted Account

In certain states, judges may require a minor's funds to be deposited into a restricted guardianship account, which can only be accessed with a court order.

Courts want to ensure the minor's funds are not used recklessly by their parents or appointed guardians. It is for this reason that courts only allow for the release of funds if they reach a certain threshold amount, and they are being used for purchases that benefit the minor (e.g., college, property, etc.).

Incapacity Planning

Years ago, I had a potential client come in for a consultation. He was a very passionate man and wanted to take conservatorship over his father who was suffering from dementia. He was concerned for his father's wellbeing, and he was his father's only living blood relative. When he arrived at my office, he was wet from the chest down, almost like he had been fly fishing in a nearby lake except there were no lakes near my office. The more I sat with him the more I realized something was very wrong. He had been estranged from his father for over 30 years and recently came down from Northern California on a Greyhound bus. He went to the memory care facility where his father was living, demanded the nurses take him off all his medications, and checked his father out from the facility. He took his father back to his father's house, changed the locks and boarded up the windows. As it turned out, the father had been married to the same woman for over 60 years and raised his stepdaughter as his own during that time. Luckily, the father had met with a well-qualified estate planning attorney a few years prior and drafted a comprehensive estate plan that explicitly excluded his son from serving in any capacity in relation to him. This avoided the son's ability to get conservatorship over his father.

Think about what would have happened to that father had he not met with a lawyer prior to his incapacitation.

The truth is, had the father not drafted his estate planning documents the way he did, the son could have dragged his case through the court system making it very difficult for any other family member to care for his needs.

Fortunately, there are ways for you to plan for your incapacity and appoint individuals you trust to manage your affairs while you are still alive but are incapable of managing your own affairs.

The easiest way to plan, is to have the following documents in place:

- Revocable Living Trust
- Durable Power of Attorney
- Healthcare Directive
- Nomination of Conservator (can be a standalone document or imbedded in your Healthcare Power of Attorney)

Property Transfers After Your Death

Shortly after your death, your property or assets will be transferred to your beneficiaries. However, the speed at which the transfer occurs depends on whether the assets are categorized as probate assets or non-probate assets.

Distinguishing between probate and non-probate assets can save you years of court delays and related costs. Understanding the distinction is important.

Probate Assets

These are assets that must go through a court-supervised probate process. Ownership of these assets can only be transferred from the deceased owner to a beneficiary under this court-administered process.

Not all assets you own will go through probate. Assets titled in your name only, with no co-owner, typically require probate. This also applies to property held as tenants in common and other assets owned jointly but without rights of survivorship.

Non-probate Assets

Non-probate property is the category in which most of your assets should be. These assets avoid the probate process and save your estate time and expenses because assets are transferred to the beneficiaries relatively quickly.

Typically, non-probate assets are assets that are held in trust or jointly owned with rights of survivorship.

However, while there are obvious benefits to having non-probate assets held in joint ownership with rights of survivorship, there are some pitfalls of which to be aware.

The main pitfall is having an asset co-owned by someone who is not bound to act in the best interests of all beneficiaries. For example, your spouse may inherit your property, re-marry, and as a result, not be legally obliged to transfer the property to the other intended beneficiaries. Another scenario to plan for is if you and your spouse die together, in which case the asset will end up in probate.

The two things guaranteed in life
are death and taxes. One you see
coming, the other you don't.

Estate Taxes

We have all heard the cliché, "The two things guaranteed in life are death and taxes," unfortunately, there is truth to the statement.

The good news is that there are ways to minimize your family's tax burden after your death. Let's first explore the estate tax, (or as some call it, the "death tax").

The estate tax is a tax levied on the transfer of property from the deceased to the beneficiaries. The tax is not applied to assets transferred to a surviving spouse, which is called the unlimited marital deduction. It is important to note that the IRS does not extend the unlimited marital deduction to noncitizen spouses.

It is also worth noting that the estate tax is only levied on estates that exceed the estate and gift exemption or the lifetime exclusion prescribed by the Internal Revenue Service (IRS). As of 2022 this exemption is $12.06 million.[2]

This threshold has significantly increased over the years, increasing from $5.5 million in 2017 to $11.18 million in 2018, and $12.06 million in 2022, due to the Tax Cuts and Jobs Act of 2017.[3]

As such, only a small percentage of individuals in the U.S. are liable to pay the federal estate tax (an estimated 2,000 estates).[4] However, that tax break is set to expire and may be in jeopardy even sooner than anticipated.

The current lifetime estate and gift tax exemption amount is set to sunset (go back) to a reduced amount in the year 2025.

---

[2] IRS Publication Rev. Proc. 2019-44
[3] P.L. 115-97, 115th Congress (2017-2018). H.R.1 - *An Act to provide for reconciliation pursuant to titles II and V of the concurrent resolution on the budget for fiscal year 2018.*
[4] Washington Post (2017). *3,200 wealthy individuals wouldn't pay estate tax next year under GOP plan.*

Estate taxes have been eliminated for several families and households; however, some people do have to worry about this tax. Thus, estate tax planning is an important and critical part of your estate plan. Any asset that is transferred above the lifetime exclusion amount is currently taxed at the 40% bracket.

When planning your estate, there are several types of taxes that should be considered and planned. Estate taxes are just the big common question most people ask about.

CHAPTER 2
YOUR BENEFICIARIES

Plans are nothing:
Planning is everything.

— Dwight D. Eisenhower

W hether you take the time to name a beneficiary for your estate or not, someone is bound to inherit your assets. That someone *could* very well be the state. If you do not designate your beneficiaries in a Will, or some other written instrument, the state will find your heirs through *intestate succession*. The state conveniently left itself on the list to inherit, albeit at the bottom of the list.

Taking the time to name a beneficiary makes sure your assets will pass as per your wishes. It also allows you to have some control from the grave, if that is what you want. Although you must keep in mind there are laws restricting how long you can control from the grave. Eventually the assets must pass to a beneficiary.

───────────── 🌳 ─────────────

Taking the time to name a beneficiary makes sure
your assets will pass as per your wishes.

There are several benefits to naming beneficiaries to your estate, such as:

Certainty: Assigning a beneficiary to your estate (whether partially or fully) provides certainty about who will inherit your assets. This gives you the peace of mind that your loved ones will be looked after following your death.

<u>Efficiency</u>: Assigning beneficiaries to your estate means that your beneficiaries will inherit your assets soon after your death. If done properly, your loved ones will not have to go through a tedious and often drawn-out probate process.

<u>Keeping it in the family</u>: Choosing beneficiaries will often protect the assets you spent your lifetime acquiring and preserving. Assigning beneficiaries means you may provide for your children and your children's children, resulting in generational wealth that continues long after you have gone.

<u>Protection</u>: Not every beneficiary you name is going to be able to inherit assets upon your passing, even if they think they are. Some beneficiaries need added protection drafted into their distributions to protect them from creditors, or their own poor judgment.

You may already have an idea of who you want to name as your beneficiary; however, for some people planning distributions is not as easy as you would think.

As we explore, we should look at the two types of beneficiaries for which you need to prepare: primary and contingent beneficiaries.

Primary Beneficiaries

In deciding on your primary beneficiaries, you should consider those closest to you or whom you want to inherit first. If you are married with children, this will often be your spouse and your children, but not always. If you are not married and have no children or close relatives, there are other options.

It is not uncommon for a person to name a charity to inherit their assets. In some cases, incorporating a tax-exempt entity can have tax saving benefits. You can name a charitable organization, a school, or even a corporation as your beneficiary. You can even name Fido as your beneficiary (it has been done before). The choice is yours.

In deciding on beneficiaries, you can also stipulate various distribution methods, including the per stirpes or per capita method.

Per stirpes designation is a method whereby if a named beneficiary dies before you, the children, grandchildren, or great-grandchildren of the beneficiary are entitled to inherit the deceased beneficiary's portion of the estate. It also ensures your legacy lives on through the descendants of the heir who predeceased you.

Per capita designation splits your estate equally among all living beneficiaries. This is often determined in your will or trust. Should a beneficiary die before you, the estate is split among the remaining beneficiaries. For example, your estate would only pass to your then-living children and would exclude any grandchildren from a deceased child.

Whomever you decide to name as your primary beneficiary, make sure your intention to leave specific assets or sums to any beneficiary is well documented. In fact, before committing to the will or trust, I suggest listing all your property and assigning these to one or more designated beneficiaries. Consider all avenues (i.e., per stirpes or per capita) and then discuss your decision with your attorney.

Contingent Beneficiaries

Determining the name of your contingent beneficiary is just as important as whom you designate as a primary beneficiary.

In the event your primary beneficiary cannot or does not want to inherit your estate, a contingent beneficiary moves into first position. This may happen if the primary beneficiaries cannot be located, dies before you, are legally incapable of inheriting, or flat out refuse the inheritance (sounds crazy, but it happens).

So, you need to carefully consider who your contingent beneficiary will be. It is worth noting that the individuals you select as contingent beneficiaries must be legally able to take possession of your estate after you die. Otherwise, it defeats the purpose of having a beneficiary.

Failing to select a contingent beneficiary may result in your estate being settled by the courts and we both know that is the last thing you want for your loved ones.

Changing Your Beneficiaries

As your life and circumstances change, you may decide to revise your list of primary and/or contingent beneficiaries. There is nothing stopping you from doing so and the process is relatively straightforward.

People typically change their beneficiaries because of events like marriage, a loved one's death, the birth of children, or divorce.

If you decide to make changes, make sure you seek the advice of a qualified estate planning attorney immediately.

Potential Conflicts Among Beneficiaries

If you and your attorney fail to anticipate problems and do not deal with them proactively, difficult issues may arise between beneficiaries, the executor, and the courts.

It is not uncommon to have a significant amount of fighting within families because they misinterpret the intentions of the will or trust and disagree about how the estate should be distributed. Add tax complexities around IRAs or other retirement accounts, a prolonged probate process, and you have a recipe for hostility among family members and overall angst.

That is why you need to work with attorneys now, so together, both of you can assess each scenario that may arise in the future and plan accordingly.
I hear families tell me every day about how close they are, and how loving everyone is toward one another. Unfortunately, I have also seen how often that is not the case after a loved one dies.

Some of the most common complications relating to beneficiaries are discussed below.

Beneficiaries Who are Minors

Complexities may arise if you designate a minor child as a primary or contingent beneficiary, as they will not be able to legally possess the assets until age 18 or 21, depending on your state's law. In this situation, a legal guardian must be appointed to manage the finances of the minor until they come of age.

Your estate plan needs to stipulate what assets are being left to minors and to what extent. It should specify who will manage their finances and at what age you deem the minor fit to manage their own inheritance responsibly. The most efficient way to leave an inheritance to a minor is by creating a trust for their benefit.

Choice of Executor

Whom you nominate as the executor of your will is pivotal; that person will be responsible for carrying out your wishes after your death.

The role of an executor is fiduciary, meaning they are required to act in the best interests of the estate and the beneficiaries of the will.

Should your executor fail to act in accordance with your wishes, your family or other beneficiaries have the legal right to challenge the executor's actions in court.

Because executors are often family members, and in most instances also beneficiaries, they must take extra care handling perceived conflicts of interest. Executors who address issues fairly and transparently can avoid any beneficiaries' grounds for objection.

Ambiguous Intentions

Misinterpretation of a deceased's intentions create conflict and often arise when estate plans are not revised to address changes in the law and changes in family dynamics. Personal circumstances, or circumstances of your beneficiaries, may change over time and need to be addressed within your estate plan.

It is important for you to communicate clearly and completely with your estate planning attorney to prevent confusion and to minimize disagreements among your beneficiaries.

Fraud or Undue Influence

Sadly, as people reach advanced ages, they sometimes fall prey to untrustworthy opportunists. For example, let us say an individual is living in an assisted living facility or a nursing home. An aide or caregiver may convince the resident to grant them power of attorney. An unscrupulous person in possession of that power of attorney could squander all the money in the resident's accounts. It happens.

Some Solutions...

While the complications outlined above are not uncommon, here are steps that your family or beneficiaries can take to address them:

- Take the issue to court. Inevitably, litigation is a tedious, emotional, and costly avenue. However, in some cases this may be the only way forward to address instances of perceived inequality.

- Seek legal mediation outside of court. An attorney can act as a mediator between parties to reach a mutually agreeable outcome.

Preventing the problem is better than solving it!

Take a proactive approach to your estate planning with constant reviews and, if required, revisions to the paper if circumstances change.

By actively managing your affairs now, you not only diminish the likelihood of conflict for your beneficiaries, but you also save them time and money. After all, isn't time the most precious resource?

Disinheritance

Disinheriting a family member can be emotional and have a damaging impact on your relationship with loved ones. It can also sow the seeds of long-lasting resentments between family members after you are gone.

In cases where a person making a Will decides to disinherit a family member, it often involves cutting one or more of the children from the Will. If, after serious consideration, you decide to take such a step, keep in mind that the law applies restrictions to prevent certain disinherited heirs from becoming wards of the state. It is almost impossible to disinherit a minor child. Courts will often require that estate funds provide for the care of minors until they reach legal age, as a form of parental financial support.

Before going down the disinheritance road, let us look at a few ways to limit your child's inheritance in a way that will be a win-win for everyone.

Revise your Revocable Living Trust

You can have a revocable living trust set up to determine what sums are transferred to your child, when those funds are transferred, and under what conditions the transfers are made. Your designated trustee can transfer funds at a rate and in an amount, you dictate in the paperwork. These transfers can also be limited to specific uses, like paying bills or college tuition, for example.

As an incentive for your child, you can also decide to direct additional funds to be transferred in the event your child reaches specific milestones, such as getting a graduate degree, getting married, or having children. You can also empower your trustee to release all the trust's principle to your child if your child satisfies certain criteria.

Leave a Modest Inheritance

Rather than completely disinherit your child or loved one, consider leaving them something of value in your will or trust. This will ensure your beneficiary is uplifted to some extent, and it can reduce the likelihood of continued family hostility.

Make Your Intentions Clear

If, for any reason, you decide to disinherit your child, ensure your intentions are crystal clear in your will or trust. Some states have laws that presume you accidentally disinherited a child. The terms of your will or trust must leave no doubt that you intended to disinherit one of your children. This will avoid any confusion or ambiguity when it comes time to transfer the assets to other beneficiaries.

This same clarity is required if you choose to disinherit other beneficiaries, not just children. The person making the will should specify that it is their intention to leave the beneficiary nothing and that the beneficiary's disinheritance is not an oversight.

When articulating the reasons for the disinheritance, it is best not to include too much detail. Remember that once a will is probated, it becomes a public record. It should use general language, perhaps noting that the beneficiary is financially independent, or that the reason for the disinheritance is well known to the beneficiary. Sometimes, too many details can create grounds for the disinherited heir to contest the will. They may be able to claim that the details used to justify disinheriting them are either false or mistaken. Be clear but discrete.

Talk it Over

Disinheriting a close family member should not be done lightly. There are several other paths you can consider that may help you resolve a conflict causing you to disinherit an heir.

Seek Counseling or Mediation

Whatever the source of a family's disagreement, if it persists and threatens to end a close relationship, I suggest seeking counseling or mediation immediately. The mediation process encourages open dialogue and provides each party with understanding of the other person's feelings.

Many attorneys are trained mediators and can serve in this role without bias. The mediator does not settle the matter or make decisions. Good mediators simply help the parties listen to each other's point of view and try to find common ground.

Offer Incentives

People almost always act if a reward is promised. So, why not offer an incentive to the child, spouse, or other family member whose decisions or behavior you wish to influence.

You can also create incentive trusts which effectively release funds upon the achievement of a milestone or criteria.

For example, if one of your children suffers from alcoholism, you could include a provision that restricts any distribution to them unless they have achieved one year of sobriety and completed a treatment program. Your trustee would be tasked with ensuring your wishes are carried out and your beneficiary would not receive any funds until they meet your benchmarks.

Assess Your Relationship with Your Beneficiary

Time can heal wounds and provide healthy perspective. For example, you may have initially disapproved of your daughter's husband or someone in his family. However, if your daughter is expecting her first child, this may be a good opportunity to address any historic frictions that exist.

When a divisive conflict with a family member is resolved, you should revise your estate plan to ensure your beneficiaries will be taken care of after you die.

Assess your overall relationship with loved ones, and as a result, consider how this may impact your estate plan. When a divisive conflict with a family member is resolved, you should revise your estate plan to ensure your beneficiaries will be taken care of after you die.

The last thing you want is to disinherit someone, make amends and forget to adjust the will appropriately. As such, we strongly suggest assessing your estate plan at every milestone or major change in circumstances in your life.

Disinheriting a Beneficiary

After considering the alternatives, if your mind is settled on disinheriting a child or another beneficiary, be sure to check the beneficiary designations on all your accounts. This includes your retirement accounts, bank accounts, investments, and other property. Ensure the transfers that will occur upon your death are still as you want them. This is something your attorney will discuss with you to confirm your estate plan is up to date.

Leaving Property When You Do Not Have Children

If you do not have children, there are several ways to structure your beneficiaries. It is equally as important for you to proactively manage your estate's affairs and life following your death.

If you do not prepare an estate plan, your estate may well go to someone you'd rather it didn't go to, or it could be transferred in a way you would not approve. With no will or next of kin, you run the risk of having your assets escheated, i.e., taken by the state, a scenario no one wants. Anyone, anything, but NOT the state!

There is a myriad of options available to childless individuals and we'll go through a couple of these in this section.

Gifting to Relatives

If you do not have children, you may have nieces, nephews, cousins, or other relatives with whom you have a close bond. You may consider them as suitable heirs to your estate. Should you decide to go down this path, make sure to specify your wishes in your will, living trust, and other estate documents.

Charities

Another option that many people choose is a gift to charity. You may decide that you would like to use your estate to give back in a big way to a cause you're passionate about.

There are several methods available if you want your estate to benefit one or more charities.

Charitable Remainder Trusts

These trusts entitle the donor, or grantor (in this case yourself), an immediate charitable tax deduction. This charitable deduction is calculated on the market value of the assets that have been transferred to the trust. Under this trust structure, the donor also receives an income from the trust until death. Then the assets are transferred to the deceased's nominated charity.

Donor-Advised Funds

Under this scenario, the donor makes tax-deductible contributions of cash, securities, or other non-cash assets to a trust. The donor can then invest those funds for potential growth and recommend grants to certain charities exempt from federal income taxes under section 501(c)(3) of the United States Code.

Private Foundations

Private foundations are common among the wealthy. These charitable organizations are often founded by one or more family members pursuant to a tax-deductible gift. These foundations are often managed by a board of directors or trustees who decide on the distribution and management of all assets held within the trust.

Friends/Business Associates

You can consider gifting your estate to close friends or business partners. You may consider certain friends as close as family, or you may have had some long-standing professional relationships that go beyond business.

If you want to ensure these friends or business associates receive the benefits from your estate, be sure you articulate the gift you want to leave and to whom with great particularity. Clearly stating your wishes will prevent your will from being contested in the courts.

CHAPTER 3
CHILDREN

Estate planning is an important and everlasting gift you can give your family. And setting up a smooth inheritance isn't as hard as you might think.

— Suze Orman

I t is hard for your children to imagine life without you and being gone yourself is difficult for us to imagine. For me personally, the guidance I give to other families every day took on new meaning when I had my first child. I could not shake the thought, "What if I'm not here to raise him?"

The hard reality is that life is unpredictable; and what is worse than leaving this world with no plan to protect and provide for your children?

Planning for your child's inheritance is a huge part of estate planning, and there are several strategies and pitfalls of which you need to be aware. Without an understanding of how to best protect your child's future today, you may open them up to a world of legal pain and financial deprivation in the future.

Your family's financial future can be adversely impacted by poor planning and lack of foresight. Life's too short for those types of mistakes, so I have devoted a whole chapter to caring for your children.

Reading this chapter will make you appreciate the optimum way to structure your estate plan so that it protects your assets in the long term and, importantly, ensures your children benefit from your lifetime of hard work for years to come.

Choosing a Guardian/Conservator for Young Children

Your estate plan needs to articulate precisely how your children will be looked after once you are gone.

If you have minor children, the starting point is to name a guardian that will look after your children until they come of age. You cannot assume your spouse will live long after you are gone, so you need to cover all contingencies and not just name one guardian and conservator. Name a couple of them.

Nominating a backup guardian and financial conservator ensures that your children have security in the unlikely event that something happens to the primary guardian or conservator. Typically, the guardian and conservator are the same person, however you can select two individuals to occupy the roles.

As part of nominating someone to care for your young children, it is also wise to select a trustee. Sometimes this trustee is your spouse, but again, a backup plan is highly recommended in case unforeseen or tragic events occur.

Once selected, your will should clearly identify the person or persons you nominate as the guardian of your minor children. By following this instruction, you will eliminate any uncertainty as to who will step into the shoes of your children's guardian.

The big question remains: "Whom do I select as the guardian/conservator of my children?"

To answer this question, the following factors should be considered:

What is the Age of the Candidate?

This problem can be a Catch-22. On one hand, an older candidate may be in a great financial situation to provide for your children in your absence. However, given their age, they may lack the stamina and fail to appreciate current parenting methods.

A younger guardian may be more in tune with the latest parenting trends and connect more on an emotional level with your children. However, their financial situation may be worse off than the older guardian candidate, and they may also have their own young children to look after.

What are Your Candidate's Values and Beliefs?

Think about your candidate's religious beliefs. Do they align with yours? What are their values about education, work, and relationships? Again, do they match yours? Since your children will be influenced by your guardian's approach to life and their ideals, these are pivotal questions to ask.

How are the Candidate's Parenting Skills?

Are they already experienced parents, or will this be a new venture for them? I suggest you see how they engage with your children during play time. If they have children, assess whether they are affectionate with their children, overly strict, or too lenient in your judgment. They would probably develop a similar pattern with your kids.

Where Does the Candidate Live?

If your children's prospective guardian does step into that role, your children will likely live with them. Do you like the area the guardian lives in? Are there some great options for schooling, health, and employment? Would you be comfortable if your kids lived in that area?

What is the Candidate's Financial Situation?

Is the guardian financially capable of providing for your children, or will this be a significant burden on them? The last thing you want is for your children be a heavy financial burden on another household. Although it is difficult to foresee anyone's future, is the guardian currently well employed and financially stable, or are they under pressure to meet the economic needs of their own family?

Is the Candidate's Household Stable?

Does the guardian come from a stable household or did their parents have issues? Did the guardian experience a dysfunctional upbringing? How peaceful, orderly, or happy does their home seem to you? If you don't know the answer, try to spend some time there, or learn from someone who knows the answer before you commit your children to live in an unknown environment.

Is Your Candidate Willing to Become a Guardian?

It may seem like a given, but it's important that your candidate consent to becoming so responsible for your children. Putting financial issues aside, does the guardian or their spouse have sufficient time to devote to your children?

Choosing a guardian/conservator is no easy task, but if you follow the right approach and thoroughly assess all these factors, your decision will be made in an informed manner.

At the end of the day, it all comes down to what's important to you and what you consider to be the most important quality of a prospective guardian.

Who Will Manage Your Child's Assets, and How Will They Do It?

Typically, your spouse will be named as executor of the will, or the successor trustee. They will be charged with transferring assets in accordance with your wishes. However, when, and how this happens is another question.

If you don't have an estate plan, and your spouse predeceases you, your child will inherit your estate. If the child is a minor, the assets will be managed by a guardian and all spending requests will need to be approved by the courts. This can be a very inconvenient and frustrating process for everyone involved.

Having your children own your estate outright is not an effective way to maintain wealth in your family in the long term. Children, whether minors or adults, often lack the financial maturity to manage their inheritance, so it's best to transfer your estate another way. This would also protect your assets from your children's creditors.

The most effective way to manage your children's inheritance is to create a trust that will hold the assets to be inherited once the minor comes of age, or a later time you designate. A trustee will be appointed to manage the trust and will control distributions for your child's education, health, living expenses, and overall support.

Leaving your assets in trust:

- affords you the flexibility of preserving your wealth while ensuring your children benefit from their inheritance,
- Protects your wealth from possible creditors of your children,
- Ensures the funds held in trust won't be released if your child goes through a divorce or separation. (Trust assets are not usually included in the marital estate.)

One thing is clear; having a trust should play prominently in your estate plan. Your attorney will go through the various ways in which a trust will serve you and your family.

Ways Your Trustee Can Manage the Trust

There are several ways a trustee can manage your trust to ensure your children and other beneficiaries are well served financially in a structured manner that accords with their financial literacy.

Some of the ways in which you can choose to administer the funds include:

- Limiting the annual income distributions to only investment income or a percentage of the value of the underlying trust assets,
- Paying the children's' expenses directly to vendors, for living expenses, rent, education and so on,
- Allowing the child or other beneficiary to move the assets outside the trust and to own the estate outright on the condition that specific milestones be met, or if they reach a certain age.

In truth, the choices are limitless. You can decide the how, when, and where you would like the trust's assets to be managed based on your view of how ready your child is to take ownership of your estate.

Naming Children as Beneficiaries of Life Insurance

While you may have the best intentions, listing your children as beneficiaries of your life insurance policies can create some complexities after your death. These complications can be handled if you structure your policy appropriately.

If you do decide to name your children as beneficiaries, and you die before they become of age, your children will not receive the benefits of the policy immediately. Under this scenario, the decision as to what happens with the proceeds of the insurance payout sits with the probate court.

As mentioned previously, the probate court will elect a guardian for the minor's estate and this guardian will preside over the management of your child's estate until your child reaches either 18 or 21 years of age.

This process is not only time consuming but can be costly because of the fees imposed by the court in overseeing the distribution of your assets.

There's a better way to financially provide for your children through an insurance policy that eliminates the risk of having to go through probate court. You can create a trust for the benefit of your children and name the trust as the beneficiary to your insurance policy. This method would avoid the probate court, having to name a guardian to manage your children's money, and you will be able to build in protections for your children over an extended period of time.

Nominate a Custodian

If you decide you want to designate one or more minor children as the beneficiaries of your life insurance policy, you should nominate a custodian for your children.

A custodian will operate in the same way as a guardian, managing your children's finances and accounts until they become of age. This is governed by the Uniform Transfers to Minors Act which operates substantially the same way in all states, except for South Carolina. As of the date of this writing, South Carolina follows the South Carolina Uniform Gifts to Minors Act (UGMA). A bill to repeal South Carolina's UGMA and replace with South Carolina's Uniform Transfer of Minors Act (UTMA) is currently sitting with the state's Senate Committee on Judiciary. The bill has received strong support from both the state's House and Senate.

Once the assets have been transferred to the beneficiary, a custodian will no longer be required.

Nominate a Guardian as a Contingent Beneficiary

If you are having doubts about naming your child as a beneficiary of your insurance policy, consider listing the child's guardian instead as a contingent beneficiary. Your spouse or partner would often be the primary beneficiary, and your guardian would simply be your back-up beneficiary.

I suggest you consider naming the same legal guardian you included in your estate plan as the custodian of the insurance proceeds. This ensures that the same guardian will be called upon if the need for a contingent beneficiary materializes.

It is important to note that naming your appointed guardian as the beneficiary of your insurance policy is not the ideal scenario for protecting your children. Once your appointed guardian is in receipt of the funds there is nothing legally restricting their use of the funds for the benefit of your children. Furthermore, the funds would be able to pay the liabilities and creditors of your named guardian/beneficiary. To put it more clearly, if the guardian was sued, the money you set aside for your children would be subject to that lawsuit.

Name the Trust as Beneficiary (Recommended in Most Scenarios)

Your trust can, and should, serve as a beneficiary if your children are minors or you would like to preserve their inheritance over time. Should this option be exercised, your trust will receive the insurance proceeds, and these will be managed by the trustee in accordance with the strategies you established within the trust.

Since your trust is revisable, you can decide to amend who receives what, and by when. A trust also ensures your family will avoid the probate court and all the headaches and costs involved in that process.

Leaving Property to Adult Children

Ask yourself the following questions and be honest with yourself:

- When you hit the legal age of 18 or 21, did you have a solid appreciation for money and managing finances responsibly?
- Were you planning what your life would look like in 10, 20, or 50 years?
- Did you think about the cost of a house, raising children, future debt, and college tuition fees?
- Did you find yourself facing any legal trouble in the early years of adulthood?
- Did you marry young, only to find you and your spouse weren't compatible over the long haul?

If you answered "No" to at least one of these questions, you are in good company.

The truth is our level of financial maturity increases as we age, and we become more appreciative of the best and worst ways to manage money. This includes reducing our risk to potential lawsuits and creditors.

Now think about your children and the stage of life they may be in when you die.

Thinking about this long and hard is important. It can make the difference between generational wealth and wealth that lasts a couple of years. It is for this reason that most financial experts strongly advise against releasing funds or assets to the adult children of the deceased immediately after the death.

***

A trust is as solid as a house,
until it's not.

The smart way is to structure your estate's finances in a way that provides for your adult children financially, but in stages, or at specific milestones.

Once again, the best way to do this is through a trust.

Not only will a trust protect your assets in the long term, but it will also help ward off creditor claims, protect your children from losing everything, and ensures that bad life choices don't cost your children their financial future.

A trust is as solid as a house. And its guardian is your trustee, who manages it in accordance with your strict instructions. Your instructions will be set out in detail in your living trust's controlling documents. These documents should be revisited whenever things change in your life or that of your family.

To maximize the benefits you derive from a trust, I strongly recommend speaking to your estate attorney. Your attorney has "been there, done that," when it comes to asset protection strategies. Your attorney should have experience establishing, maintaining, and operating trusts.

I am not saying that your adult children are likely to spend their inheritance quickly. We all know life throws curve balls, and despite best efforts, bad situations happen to even the best people. Does anyone plan to divorce when they first get married? Who plans a failed business or a downturn in the economy? Any one of these circumstances can derail your child's financial future.

Allowing your children to access the estate immediately will often mean that the funds are used to fulfill current or mid-term financial goals, not long term, wealth-creating goals.

Speak to your estate lawyer about the best way to address unforeseen circumstances in your child's life and spell out your approach in the trust documents and in any ancillary documentation.

CHAPTER 4
PLANNING FOR INCAPACITY

*End of life decisions should not be made
at the end of life.*

— Unknown

I n life, change is inevitable. Unfortunately, change may come to you unexpectedly.

Estate planning isn't just about planning for your mortality. It is also about planning for the possibility of becoming incapacitated. Who could have anticipated the disastrous pandemic of COVID-19? No one wants to imagine that as a possibility, but now we must consider it along with other unforeseen scenarios.

Definition of Incapacity

In the estate planning context, incapacity is defined as the inability to make your own decisions. Typically, one becomes incapacitated due to injury or a health condition, like dementia.

Should one become incapacitated, there are some critical decisions that need to be made, including decisions on:

- Medical treatment plan
- Financial affairs
- Living arrangements

Making decisions in each of these areas involves serious forethought and requires careful planning. That's where your estate plan comes in.

Any estate plan needs to incorporate plans for your potential incapacity. Sudden illness or accident can strike anyone at any time.

There are several documents you should consider incorporating into your overall estate plan. Unfortunately, estate planning isn't as cut and dry as many expect it to be. There are a myriad of situations which can occur that require separate legal documentation or a court order. Below I will go into detail regarding the various documents you can put in place to avoid needing court intervention.

Medical Decisions

The plan you create in anticipation of your incapacity should always include several specific documents. You can discuss your thoughts about each document with your attorney.

Living Will

I described this document earlier in chapter one. A Living Will document sets out the type of healthcare you want to receive, or you don't want to receive, in the event you are unconscious or unable to communicate. For example, if you are under anesthesia for a scheduled surgery and you suffer complications, this document would let your doctors know what steps you do or don't want them to take to prolong your life.

The Living Will informs the healthcare providers about whether you want them to intubate you if you can't breathe on your own power; whether you want a feeding tube to be inserted if you can't eat, etc.

This document does NOT transfer authority to another person to make your healthcare decisions for you.

This document only applies when you are living, hence the name "living will." The last will and trust documents execute your wishes after death.

Do Not Resuscitate Order (DNR)

A Do Not Resuscitate Order can be part of your living will or be prepared on a standalone basis. The document outlines the conditions under which you refuse to accept resuscitative measures. For example, if your heart stops, you may want the doctors to try chest compressions (cardiopulmonary respiration or CPR). However, you may not want them to do open-heart surgery or take other extraordinary measures to revive you.

The person you name as healthcare power of attorney should be someone you trust who will use sound judgment in making your healthcare decisions.

People who opt for a DNR are often suffering from terminal or life-threatening illnesses or have a high risk of complications from resuscitative measures. A DNR is signed by your physician.

Health Care Power of Attorney

Also known as an Advance Healthcare Directive, this document specifies a person to whom you grant the legal right to make medical choices on your behalf if you become incapable of making decisions yourself. The person you name as healthcare power of attorney should be someone you trust who will use sound judgment in making your healthcare decisions.

HIPAA Release

This document grants any person you name access to confidential medical information about your health and treatment. The HIPAA release usually names family members or other loved ones. It allows your health care providers to speak to your family about your medical condition and treatment, in the event you're unable to do so. However, this does not allow for your family members to make decisions on your behalf.

All four documents outlined above should be considered as part of your incapacity plan. Together, they answer necessary questions and reduce confusion if you are incapacitated or unable to communicate.

Financial Decisions

If you become incapacitated, your finances may seem like the least of your worries, but it is imperative to think about who will manage your affairs in the event you are unable to handle them yourself. Naming a durable power of attorney will ensure someone has the legal ability to carry on in your best interest, pay the mortgage, file your taxes, and hire care workers on your behalf.

It's wise to assess how your finances are structured, who holds certain bank and investment accounts, and who's authorized to access them.

The last thing you want is to leave your family unable to access money because you did not designate one of them as an authorized person. You need to consider your finances collectively. That means where are your funds stored, in what form, and how easy is it to access them?

Once you've mapped out your finances, it's time to articulate your wishes for managing your estate in your revocable living trust. These documents specify precisely how you intend to manage your financial affairs in the event you become incapacitated.

It is not uncommon for parents to name a child as a joint owner on an account for them to have immediate access to the funds in the event of incapacity or death. However, there are better ways to accomplish this goal. Once an individual becomes a joint owner on your account you are giving up control to half of the assets. Furthermore, if they get sued or have creditors, your account can be used to pay their debts by court order.

To protect your assets during your life, a well-drafted and fully funded revocable living trust with an accompanying durable power of attorney would give you optimal protection and security. However, it is important to note that these legal mechanisms do not protect your assets from your own creditors or lawsuits.

Changes to your Incapacity Plan

Like your will and overall estate plan, your incapacity plan should never stand still. There are some changes in your life that should serve as triggers to revisit your incapacity plan.

Consider the following:

- A change in relationship status: You may have been married or engaged when you initially prepared your incapacity plan. However, five years later you may be divorced or living with a new partner. You need to check whether your husband or wife was included in the initial incapacity plan and whether you still want to include them in the plan or replace your new partner's name instead.

- Moving to another state: Each state has different laws concerning estate and incapacity planning. I urge you to speak with a local attorney, someone familiar with the estate planning laws of your new state and see whether your initial incapacity plan needs to be revised.

- Starting a business: Running your own business is a lot of work. That is why you need to consider what will happen if you become incapacitated and can no longer work in your business. In this regard, it may be worth considering who your replacement would be and whether they would be ready to take on the challenge. I would also advise you to start a conversation with your insurance broker regarding key personnel policies that would provide financial support for your business during the interim period of finding a suitable replacement.

- <u>Having a child</u>: Having a child is the one of the greatest joys in life. If you prepared your incapacity plan before you had children, chances are you did not consider the possibility that you might not be in a condition to look after or provide for your children. In the event this happens, you will need to name a guardian to care for your children. You also need to consider if the proposed guardian will be able to care for your children both financially and emotionally.

- <u>Injury or illness</u>: If you suffer an injury or discover that you are seriously ill, it is best to reassess your incapacity plan immediately. You need to ensure your plan reflects your current and future health needs.

- <u>Age</u>: As you age, you need to reassess your medical and financial needs. As you age and circumstances change, you may need to revisit your incapacity plan to ensure your family and your future needs are covered.

As laws change over time, it is always best to speak with your attorney regularly. I would suggest meeting with your attorney at least once every three years to ensure your plan is still valid and all scenarios are covered.

Be proactive in the management of your incapacity plan.

CHAPTER 5
WILLS

*Wills are trumped by legal titles
to real estate or beneficiary
designations on financial accounts,
retirement plans, and
insurance policies.*

— Marc Faber

W e have touched on the overall concept of a will and its importance. In this chapter, we delve into a lot more information, explaining the requirements of a will, types of wills, and how they operate.

Your will is one of the most important documents of your estate plan. It determines what happens with your estate after your death should your estate be administered through the probate court. It will also be key if your estate is administered using the small estate affidavit here in California.

If the will is not ironclad, or if your wishes are unclear, it can lead to a lot of unnecessary litigation after you die. Not to mention, a poorly planned estate administration has the increased potential of forever damaging already strained family relationships.

Having a will or an estate plan in place is not as common as one would think. According to the Caring.com 2021 Wills and Estate Planning Study, the number of young adults with a will increased by 63% since the year 2020. Despite the COVID-19 pandemic, the overall percentage of Americans who have a will has not significantly changed.

One of the reasons cited for not having a will or estate planning documents is due to the lack of education or resources, rather than simple procrastination. If this is you, I applaud your effort to learn more by reading this book. I encourage you to schedule your initial consultation with an estate planning attorney to learn more about what you need to do to protect your family and loved ones.

Take a moment to think about your untimely demise and what your family's life would look like without you in it.

It is difficult to ponder your own death and to take steps now to plan for it. Take a moment to think about your untimely demise and what your family's life would look like without you in it.

Will Requirements (Last Will and Testament)

Not all wills are created equal. While you may think you have prepared a will, it is only valid if it satisfies your state's legal requirements.

Failure to comply with these requirements will have serious consequences, including possibly invalidating your will. Your estate would then be distributed according to intestacy rules, meaning as though you died without a will. Your wishes as they were recorded in the will would be ignored.

Legal requirements will vary from state-to-state, but the fundamental concepts generally apply. The fundamental concepts will be covered in this chapter.

Age of Majority

In most states, an individual must be at least 18 years old to validly execute a will.

In some circumstances, some states may permit a will to be valid even when made by a person younger than 18 years old. These exceptions include where a minor is married or serving in the U.S. Armed Forces. In Georgia, a person can make a will at the age of 14. You should always check with your lawyer to learn what the minimum age is for writing a will in your state.

Legal Capacity

The law requires that when you create your will, you are doing so knowingly and with a sound mind. To confirm this, you may be subject to a test to assess that you had/have the legal capacity to prepare a will. This test will confirm that:

- you know that you made a will,
- you understand the effects of the document, and
- you understand the components of your estate and what you are transferring at the time of your death.

Voluntary Intent

There have been instances in which an individual was coerced or was under duress when they made their will. The law ensures that a will made under these circumstances will not be accepted by a court.

You need to have intent while preparing your will and disposing of your assets upon your death. Your attorney will guide you through the process of documenting your intent in the form most preferred by the courts.

Beneficiaries

You need to nominate one or more persons, groups, or organizations that will be your beneficiaries. Specifying where you want your assets to go is the central purpose of the Last Will and Testament.

If any of your beneficiaries are minors, you also need to name a guardian or conservator. Consider drafting a testamentary trust to hold the assets for any underage or incapacitated beneficiary.

Executor

Your will should also name the executor, that is, the individual whom you want to execute your wishes. The executor is the person who will take your will to the probate court and start the probate process. Their job is to make sure all your affairs are properly addressed, creditors paid, and assets distributed to your named beneficiaries.

The executor is entitled to a fee for their services. In California, this fee is set statutory and is based on a percentage of the gross assets in the estate.

Witnesses

States vary in the number of witnesses required for a will to be valid. Many states require your witnesses be unrelated parties, and not beneficiaries under the will. Other states allow your beneficiaries to be witnesses, however it's important to check with your state's laws.

California requires two witnesses, over the age of 18 and not beneficiaries of the will.

Whoever your witnesses are, they need to sign and date the will. They may also be required to sign an affidavit that confirms their authentication of the will and their own signature.

Spouses

If you have a spouse, then you need to list what they will inherit upon your death. Generally, your spouse is protected from being disinherited. It isn't uncommon for an individual going through the divorce process to want to change their will prior to the finalization of their divorce. Unfortunately, until the divorce is final your spouse is still protected. Each state has its own laws relating to spousal rights to inherit. Check your state's laws and discuss with your lawyer.

If you would like to set limitations on the portion of your estate that is transferred to your spouse, during a period of separation you would need spousal consent absent a validly executed prenuptial or post-nuptial agreement.

Requirement of Writing

Your will must be in writing and signed by you (creator of the will). While some states acknowledge oral wills, in limited circumstances, it is not advisable to fall back on this. California is not a verbal will state.

The number of required signatures will also vary by state. Some states require the will to be signed at the end of the document, whereas others cover this by requiring the signature to be somewhere on the document. To ensure that you comply with your respective state's laws, I recommend you sign or initial every page of your will, and sign at the end.

There are strict legal requirements that you need to fulfill to create a valid will. The factors we covered in this chapter are the bare minimum. However, there may be actions you need to take depending on your individual circumstances and the state where you reside.

To cover all bases, consult with your estate attorney. Keep in mind that an improperly executed will is as good as not having a will in the first place.

Holographic (Handwritten) Will

California is a state that will recognize a handwritten will as being valid. For the handwritten will to be recognized under California law certain requirements must be met.

- The entire will must be in the testator's own handwriting.
- The date should appear at the top of the document.
- Includes statement of intent.
- Include capacity statement.

An example of a holographic will can be found on the next page.

LAST WILL AND TESTAMENT
OF
NICOLE D'AMBROGI
DATED: AUGUST 10, 2020

I, Nicole D'Ambrogi, OF SAN DIEGO, CA, USA, WRITE THIS HOLOGRAPIC WILL WITH THE INTENT OF SETTING FORTH MY WISHES FOR THE DISPOSITION OF MY ESTATE AFTER MY DEATH. AS OF THE DATE OF THIS WILL I AM OF SOUND MIND AND AM CAPABLE OF DETERMINING MY OWN AFFAIRS.

OPTIONAL THIS PARTICULAR HOLOGRAPIC WILL MAKES ANY PREVIOUSLY SIGNED WILL INVALID AND WITHOUT BINDING LEGAL FORCE.

AS TO MY PERSONAL POSSESSIONS, AND CHATTELS, WHICH I LEAVE BEHIND IN THE WAKE OF MY DEATH, I, HERE AND NOW, DECLARE MY INTENT AS TO THEIR DISPOSITION

AS TO MY WEDDING RING, I WANT IT TO GO TO MY DAUGHTER, JULIET D'AMBROGI.

AS TO MY CLASSIC CAR, I WANT IT TO GO TO MY SON, DAXTON D'AMBROGI.

Nicole D'Ambrogi
8/10/2020

Types of Wills

There are four types of wills you need to be aware of.

Simple Will

This is a generic will appropriate for an uncomplicated estate. You can complete a simple will quite easily and inexpensively. These wills are usually created by people who do not own many assets, are relatively young, or do not have enough assets to trigger probate.

Many people who call the office stating that all they need is a "simple will" come to find out they have assets that exceed the probate threshold and beneficiaries who are underage. With the free access to information, the internet has made it easy for individuals to "self-diagnose" their estate planning needs. Unfortunately, the laws are not as straight forward as one would think.

If you feel like you only need a simple will, I suggest you meet with a qualified estate planning attorney who can better assess whether your needs are simple or more complex.

Joint Wills

Like a simple single will, a joint will is signed by two or more individuals (usually a married couple) who leave their assets to each other.

Under a joint will, the surviving individual will inherit the entire estate after the first spouse dies. A joint will also directs what happens to the estate upon the later death of the second person.

The problem with a joint will, and the reason for it no longer being common, is that it cannot be changed after the first person or testator dies. This creates difficulty for the surviving testator because they cannot amend the will as their life circumstances change over time unless a court grants them permission to do so.

Some people choose a joint will precisely because it ensures the surviving testator cannot change the strategy agreed upon with the other testator regarding the distribution of assets.

A joint will can be beneficial for couples who marry late in life but who have children from previous marriages. In those cases, a joint will protects the rights of the children and ensures the wishes of their parents are preserved. Frankly speaking, I have not had a need to draft a joint will. In fact, I would favor the joint trust in this scenario due to the ability to manage assets even during life but during a period of incapacity. A will only takes effect upon the death of the creator, or the joint creators.

Testamentary Trust Will

A testamentary trust will can be a great way to protect your assets from creditors or spouses of adult children, and it can provide a tax efficient method to preserve funds for a child's education. Under this will category, one or more trusts are established, meaning your assets are protected pursuant to a trust structure.

Testamentary trust wills often consist of:

- The assets from your estate that will be transferred to each respective trust.
- Who the trustee will be for each trust.
- The beneficiaries of each trust. If you have children under the legal age, your will should also articulate how you intend the trustee to manage your assets for your children.

A testamentary trust may be a good estate planning approach for a young couple with minor children. Hypothetically, the couple may not have enough assets to trigger a probate, but there are life insurance policies for the benefit of their minor children. Naming the testamentary trust as a beneficiary will ensure the funds are held and protected for their minor children and should avoid probate or court action.

Living Will

We discussed a living will earlier in this book, but I must underscore that too many people remain unprepared for life's unpredictable challenges. Unlike a last will that becomes active only after your death, a living will is effective during your life and ensures you get the medical care you want. It provides your family with an outline of what medical treatment you want and which procedures you do not want. That knowledge relieves your family of guessing about what you want them to do when faced with end-of-life decisions.

It is for these reasons and more that I strongly recommend you get a living will as part of your overall estate plan.

However, for more specifics on this, check out Chapter 4.

Prepare Your Will

The information you need to draft your will is not extensive, but it is a good idea to be organized so you will not need to go back and forth with your attorney. Playing "info-tennis" is the last thing you want to be doing when making serious decisions affecting your family after your death. You will need the following information to best be prepared for your initial consultation with your attorney. Many law firms have intake questionnaires that will guide you through the information that is needed.

Personal Information

Personal information includes:

- your full legal name, and any former names or aliases,
- current home address,
- date of birth,
- details about your spouse and/or former spouse (i.e., name, age, etc.),
- details about your children (names, ages, etc.),
- citizenship

About Your Assets

You should list all the assets you own, including real estate, shares or interests in a business, investments, bank accounts, pensions, insurance policies, cars, and other valuable personal property or possessions.

You should assign a value to each asset. This can be determined by engaging a professional appraiser or undertaking comparative analysis. For your real estate, it is worth consulting with a realtor. For other assets, information may be more readily available (for example, stock prices).

Property

In listing properties, list the address of the property, whether you own them outright, jointly or if they are subject to mortgages, loans with financial institutions, or other encumbrances (like leases to tenants). It is very helpful if you know the Assessor Parcel Number (APN) for your property. This will assist your attorney in pulling any needed property records.

Investments

List all investments held by you or jointly with another individual or business entity. Investments can include stocks, bonds, insurance policies, shares of a business, savings accounts, mutual funds, and so on.

For each investment you need to document the following:

- the name of the entity in which you are invested, and its contact details,
- the policy and/or account number(s),
- the number and value of shares in the company,
- share certificate numbers, and if possible, a copy of the certificates and any related documents or addenda.

Personal Possessions

Personal possessions you should list include things with more than nominal financial or sentimental value. These can include art collections, jewelry, vehicles, furniture, electronics, and collectibles.

It is also important to identify any specific gifts to individuals. In my holographic will example, I bequeathed my wedding ring to my daughter and my classic car to my son. Making specific gifts of real and personal property reduces the chances of disagreements among heirs.

Business Assets

These are assets you hold with a business that you own individually or jointly under another corporate structure.

Business assets can include, land, buildings and other structures, fixtures, and fittings (for the business premises), operating equipment and machinery, registered patents and domain names, goodwill, bank accounts, etc.

As part of this information, you need to document the extent to which you own these assets and their market value.

Debts

In calculating your total net worth and estate, your attorney needs to calculate your debts. Typical debts include bank loans, mortgages, credit cards, and private loans owed to other parties (for e.g., to other family members).

Digital Assets

It may seem strange to think that your digital life can affect your will, but if you have conducted business online or made money via social media, music, or publishing, that money should be included in your documentation.

Documenting digital assets is becoming a challenge for attorneys due to problems accessing digital accounts that are password protected. So, it is wise to provide as much information as possible about these accounts to your lawyer. This information can include the assets you hold, their location, and anything else your attorney deems relevant.

If you have an online vault that stores your usernames and passwords it is worth looking into naming an individual to gain access upon your incapacity or death. This way someone would be able to access your accounts for administration purposes and it would make it easier to identify all of your online accounts as well.

Beneficiaries

Provide as much information about your beneficiaries as possible. This includes names (include any alias, maiden names, or AKAs), contact details, current marital status, and dependents.

At this stage, before you meet with your lawyer, think about how you would like to distribute your estate and to whom.

Guardians

If your children are still minors, you need to nominate a guardian to manage your estate in the event you die before they reach the age of majority. As part of this important information, you need to provide the guardian's full name, contact details, your relationship with them, and other information your attorney might request.

Before nominating a guardian for your children, take the time to find out if that person is willing to accept that responsibility. If you name a guardian who is unwilling or unable to accept the role, the court may be forced to name someone whom you would not have approved.

Trusts

If you already have established trusts, list these in detail. Include details of the trustee, beneficiaries, and the trust's overall purpose.

If you have a consultation scheduled, notify your attorney as they will likely want to review any prior wills or trusts.

Checklist

To make the above information more digestible, I have created a checklist on the following page that summarizes the information you need to collect for your will.

Information for Your Will
CHECKLIST

PERSONAL INFORMATION

_____ Your full name, any formal name(s) or alias(es), maiden names, etc.
_____ Current home address(es)
_____ Date of birth
_____ Citizenship
_____ Personal information details of your spouse (i.e., name, age, date of birth, citizenship status)
_____ Your children's information (names, addresses, dates of birth, etc.)

YOUR ASSETS

_____ Real property deeds
_____ Investment accounts
_____ Personal possessions
_____ Business assets
_____ Debts
_____ Digital Assets
_____ Pets

BENEFICIARIES

_____ Contact details
_____ Current marital status
_____ Depends
_____ Date of birth
_____ Citizenship

GUARDIANS

_____ Contact details
_____ Responsibilities
_____ Relationship

TRUSTS

_____ Trustee contact details
_____ Intent of the trust
_____ Beneficiaries
_____ Conditions for minor children or beneficiaries

Challenges to Your Will

Actor and stage performer, Patrick Swayze, reportedly signed a last will and testament prior to his death. However, after his passing his family members contested the will on multiple grounds. They argued that the signature was forged, and that he was not of sound mind at the time of signature.

Jimi Hendrix died without a will, and his estate was the center of bitter litigation between his brother and stepsister for more than 45 years.

Celebrity probate sagas are interesting to follow, but unfortunately the intense arguments and raw emotions of probate litigation are a common thread among family members engaged in probate litigation.

If a will is properly drafted, it is unlikely that a will challenge will be successful. However, there are some circumstances in which a will can be challenged successfully.

The most common sources of will contests are discussed below.

Testamentary Capacity

The testamentary capacity of a person leaving a will can be challenged on two grounds:

The Age of The Testator

You may recall that only someone who reaches the age of majority is legally competent to create a valid will. The only exceptions may be if the individual is married or serves in the U.S. military.

If an unmarried minor who is not in the U.S. military creates a will, a prospective heir will probably succeed in legally challenging the will's validity.

The Mental Capacity of The Testator

If a person contesting a will can prove by clear and convincing evidence that the testator did not understand that they were making a will, or was suffering from some delusion, then the court may find the testator lacked the mental capacity to create a will. Such a finding would invalidate the will.

To determine whether the testator was of sound mind and judgement when creating the will, the court will assess whether the individual understood the following:

- the purpose and function of a will,
- that the will dictates the distribution of their estate,
- the value and components of the estate, and
- the beneficiaries.

Multiple Versions of a Will

Typically, the courts will favor the most recent version of a will. To remove any possible doubt as to which version of the will you intend to be binding, your lawyer will always include language declaring that you renounce and revoke all previous wills and codicils and that you intend the current will to be binding. Failing to clearly identify which document is your "Last Will and Testament" virtually guarantees a court challenge to its validity.

Witness Signatures

Signing and dating your will in the presence of witnesses, who also sign the will in each other's presence is a standard, basic requirement. Each state has its own statutory rules about the number of witnesses needed to create a valid will.

The absence of the required number of witness signatures can become a basis for the will to be contested and be deemed null and void.

If a will fails to contain required provisions,
it may not be considered valid.

Insufficient Information

If a will fails to contain required provisions, it may not be considered valid.

While each state has its own laws about what constitutes a valid will, at minimum a will must:

- confirm that the will is that of the testator,

- specify the assets to be distributed upon death,

- nominate an executor who will manage the distribution of the assets in accordance with the testator's wishes, and

- specify the beneficiaries, and if required, guardians for minor children.

Your attorney can assist by ensuring your will contains necessary details and complies with all your state's laws.

CHAPTER 6
LIVING TRUSTS

Do something today that your future self will thank you for.

— Sean Patrick Flanery

E state planning is not just about what will happen after you die. Estate planning is about controlling your assets now, so that you can focus on what is most important.

Living trusts, like other trusts, serve as invaluable vehicles through which you can protect your assets and dictate how you want your wealth to be distributed.

Under a living trust, your assets are placed into a trust for your benefit during your lifetime. Upon death, your assets are then managed and/or transferred to beneficiaries by the trustee you designated in the trust documents. This individual is called a "successor trustee." Their role is similar in nature to the appointed executor of your will; however, the successor trustee does not have to open a probate to administer the trust after your passing.

A living trust avoids the probate process and its associated costs and delays. With only a will, your estate will go through court proceedings. A living trust, on the other hand, means your assets can be transferred immediately after your death to your designated beneficiaries.

The cost of preparing and creating a living trust is only a fraction of what an uncontested probate proceeding would be. If the probate proceeding is contested, the entire estate may be drained to pay the legal fees, leaving your heirs empty handed and broken hearted.

A living trust is a private document, not open to public scrutiny like a will going through probate court. Your assets are distributed in private as per your wishes.

How a Living Trust Works

A revocable living trust functions differently at different times in your life. We refer to the person making the trust as the trustor or grantor. The trustor is the one who creates the trust and set the rules for successor trustees and beneficiaries to abide by. Typically, the trustor reserves certain powers within the trust during the trustor's lifetime. The trust functions differently among three common scenarios: during your lifetime, if you become incapacitated, and upon your death.

During Your Life

During this period, you, as the trustor, can manage the assets of your revocable living trust as you see fit. Oftentimes, the trustor is the initial trustee during their lifetime, making decisions on how the assets held by the trust are to be managed. A trustor may even revoke a revocable living trust if the trustor finds it necessary. Revoking the trust might occur if there were a divorce, an illness, or a different trust was created.

A revocable living trust shares the same tax identification or social security number as the trustor. Because the trust is revocable, the IRS continues to view the assets as belonging to the trustor, since the trustor has retained dominion and control over the trust assets. The trust's tax returns are often filed on the trustors Form 1040.

If Incapacitated

If you become incapacitated, the terms of your revocable living trust will guide the management of your assets.

The trust agreement also confirms your successor trustee will step in and manage your estate on your behalf, but in accordance with your wishes.

A revocable living trust is an important document and protects your assets from being squandered during your incapacity and ensures your wishes will be followed. Using a revocable trust also eliminates some common risks, such as a relative who might otherwise have unfettered access to the accounts of an incapacitated person.

Upon Death

Upon your death, a revocable living trust converts to an irrevocable trust. Since you, as the trustor, were the only person who could revoke or amend the terms of the trust, your death renders permanent the terms existing at the time of your passing.

Once this happens, your successor trustee steps in to carry out the terms you set forth in the event of your death. This will often include instructions about paying debts, taxes, transferring assets and property to beneficiaries and in what manner.

Living Trusts and Taxes

Depending on your stage of life and the way you chose to structure your living trust, the tax implications of living trusts can vary. The discussion below is simply a guide and should not be construed as legal or tax advice. You should always consult with licensed attorneys and tax professionals when making important decisions in this area.

Your living trust structure will have an impact on your tax liability. There are three main taxes to consider: income tax, gift/estate tax, and capital gains tax.

Income Tax Consequences

Generally, if you, as the trustor, serve as trustee of your own trust, the income from your living trust's assets will be reported on your individual income tax return or Form 1040.

The trust's tax identification number will be the same as your own social security number because you control the assets in the trust, and you still stand to benefit. However, a separate tax identification number may be assigned if you become mentally incapacitated and your successor trustee takes over. The IRS will issue the trust an employer identification number (EIN).

Of course, if you want to obtain an EIN while still capable and healthy, you are free to do so. The trust simply becomes identified as a separate but associated entity with its own tax return, using IRS form 1041.

I urge you to check with your tax professional or attorney to understand the best means of managing your tax affairs, and determine what options produce the most tax-efficient outcome.

Gift Tax Consequences

Upon your death, your trust may be subject to federal or state gift taxes.

Generally, a gift tax will be levied on gifts or monies transferred to beneficiaries that exceed $16,000 per year as of 2022. Any amount gifted that exceeds the annual exclusion dips into your lifetime exclusion limit. As of this writing in 2022, the federal lifetime exclusion limit for gifts is $12.06 million. So, most people do not need to worry about giving away more than they are permitted without tax liability. But there are many among us who are wealthy enough for this to be a factor in their decision making.

The gift and estate tax exemption will sunset at the end of December 31, 2025, to $5 million per person.

It is also important to note that under the current law, the gift and estate tax exemption will sunset at the end of December 31, 2025, to $5 million per person, adjusted for inflation.

Estate Tax Consequences

We will discuss estate taxes in a separate chapter; however, it is worth noting that a revocable living trust is taxed in the same way as a will. The chief benefit of having a living trust in this regard is to avoid an expensive and inconvenient probate process.

But, like the gift tax, the estate tax is only levied on estates valued more than the current limit of $12.06 million. As such, the estate tax does not impact many Americans upon the transfer of assets following a death, for now.

Joint Revocable Living Trust for Married Couples

There are several benefits to holding your assets in a joint revocable living trust with your spouse. With that said, the joint trust is not a one size fits all and may not be the right fit for your financial and marital situation.

Benefits:

- **Administrative Ease:** A joint revocable trust is easy to fund, manage and maintain over the joint lifetime of both spouses. All assets are in the same trust and the terms, conditions, and wishes of all parties are reflected in one set of trust documents.
- **Cost effective:** Having one trust that you and your spouse manage reduces the cost and attorney's fees involved in administering separate trusts.
- **Asset splitting:** If your main asset is your home, it would be difficult to split between two trusts. A joint trust would allow for the asset to be held in one trust.

Drawbacks:

- **Asset Protection:** Having a joint revocable living trust does not protect your assets from your spouse or their creditors. There is no asset protection in a revocable living trust, there is only probate avoidance protection.

- **Second marriages or separate lives:** There is a way for you to split your revocable living trust in two parts upon the first spouse to die; however, this can cause a lot of administration frustration for the surviving spouse and successor trustee.

- **Conflicting Interests:** When two people enter a marriage many of their interests are merged with their spouse; however, that does not include their legal rights. Spouses can have differing opinions when it comes to beneficiaries and trust structure. In these scenarios it may be advisable for the parties to establish their own separate trusts to ensure their interest in the property is distributed per their wishes under the law.

The decision to establish a joint trust or separate trust is best discussed with your estate planning attorney. Your attorney will be able to review your assets, answer questions regarding the current characterization of property, and help identify goals and pitfalls of both methods.

10 Most Common Trusts

Below are the ten most common types of specific trusts to help you and your family protect your assets and plan where, and how, you want the assets distributed.

1.   **Bypass Trust.** Commonly referred to as a credit shelter trust, family trust, or B trust, a bypass trust contains a portion of a deceased spouse's accounts and property and uses the deceased spouse's lifetime exclusion amount to reduce or eliminate estate tax. Because the estate tax is calculated at the first spouse's death, this trust is bypassed for estate tax purposes at the second spouse's death.

2.   **Charitable Lead Trust.** One way to leave money to your favorite charities is with a charitable lead trust. This provides a stream of income to your charity for a specific period of years or a lifetime. At the end of the period, or at death, whatever is left goes to you or your loved ones with significant tax savings.

3.   **Charitable Remainder Trust.** A charitable remainder trust is a trust which provides a stream of income to the beneficiaries for a period of years or a lifetime. At the end of the period, the remainder goes to the charity. There can be significant tax savings as well.

4.   **Special Needs Trust.** A special needs trust allows you to provide money or property for the benefit of someone with special needs without disqualifying them from receiving governmental benefits. Federal laws allow

special needs beneficiaries to receive certain types of benefits from a carefully crafted trust *without* defeating eligibility for government benefits.

5.   Generation-Skipping Trust. A generation-skipping trust allows you to distribute your money and property to your grandchildren, or even to later generations, without taxation, by using your lifetime exemption to offset any tax that could be due.

6.   Grantor Retained Annuity Trust. A grantor retained annuity trust is an irrevocable trust which provides you with an annuity for a specific amount of time, based on the value of the property in the trust. Upon completion of the annuity period, the remaining money and property are transferred to those you have named. This type of trust is used to make large financial gifts to your loved ones of accounts or property that are expected to grow in value at a higher rate than the annuity rate being paid back to you.

7.   Irrevocable Life Insurance Trust. An irrevocable life insurance trust is designed to own high-value life insurance and receive the payment of the death benefit upon the trust maker's death. The main advantage is that the life insurance proceeds are excluded from the deceased's estate for tax purposes. However, the proceeds are still available to provide liquidity to pay taxes, equalize inheritances, fund buy-sell agreements, or provide an inheritance.

8.   Marital Trust. A marital trust is designed to protect the accounts and property for the surviving spouse's benefit, and also qualify for the unlimited marital deduction. These accounts and pieces of property are excluded from estate tax at the first spouse's death but are included in his or her estate for tax purposes.

9.   Qualified Terminable Interest Property Trust (QTIP). A qualified terminable interest property trust initially provides income to the surviving spouse, and, upon the surviving spouse's death, the remaining money and property are distributed to other named beneficiaries. The trust is still allowed to qualify for the unlimited marital deduction. This is often used in second marriage situations and to maximize estate and generation-skipping tax exemptions and tax planning flexibility.

10.   Testamentary Trust. A testamentary trust is a trust created in a will upon the individual's death. It is commonly used to protect the money and property on behalf of a beneficiary as opposed to transferring the money and property to the beneficiary outright. This type of trust can help when a beneficiary is too young to manage their own money or property, has medical or drug issues, or may be incapable of responsibly managing their own money. The trust can also provide asset protection from lawsuits, or a claim by a divorcing spouse brought against the beneficiary. Unlike a revocable living trust or an irrevocable trust, where property should be transferred into a trust during the trust maker's lifetime to work property and avoid probate, testamentary trusts require the sometimes lengthy and expensive probate process before the trust is created.

Preparing Your Living Trust

The information you need to prepare a living trust is similar to what you gathered to prepare for your will. Oftentimes your attorney will send you an intake questionnaire prior to your consultation that will have you fill out all the information needed prior to your appointment. Ensuring you complete your intake form in as much detail as possible helps the attorney ensure the time spent during the consultation is focused on your substantive questions and concerns. This will allow the attorney to be in the best position possible to answer all the questions you have about your estate.

In preparation for your appointment with your attorney, begin by gathering the following information:

Personal Information About You

This is the same personal information you would have to collect for your will, including your name, address, date of birth, social security number, citizenship status, marital status, date of birth, etc. Your attorney will also need this information for your spouse and your children.

List All Your Assets

This list should be as comprehensive as possible. List all your assets, account numbers (imperative for proper funding) and their value. Assets in your list should include all the following:

- real estate portfolio,
- stocks and/or bonds,
- business investments,
- bank accounts,
- life or other insurance policies,
- vehicles,
- jewelry or art collection
- anything else you prescribe some monetary or sentimental value to.

Collect All the Paperwork

Each of your assets should have some document indicating your ownership. It is important that you try to gather deeds of title, certificates, policy documents, certificates of authenticity (for personal belongings), registration details, and similar evidence for each asset. This paperwork will be shared with your attorney and kept on file. These documents ultimately assist the attorney in helping you transfer the title of the asset into the name of the trust.

Select the Beneficiaries

This may be relatively straightforward for you since your beneficiaries typically match those identified in your will. As part of this process, think about the portion of your estate that will go to each beneficiary and under what conditions, if any. Some beneficiaries may be able to receive an outright distribution while other beneficiaries may need to have a more conservative and protected distribution plan.

Any concerns you have should be discussed with your attorney. Many clients who love their beneficiaries and want to provide for them have very valid concerns about their beneficiaries' futures.

A well-qualified estate planning attorney will help you develop a distribution plan that accomplishes your goals and protects your beneficiaries, either from themselves or from third party creditors or spouses.

Choose a Successor Trustee

You need to decide which person or organization will manage your assets if you become incapacitated or upon your death. Your successor trustee will manage your estate according to your instructions, pay debts, distribute income, and manage all estate-related matters. You need to choose wisely here. The successor trustee should also be named as your financial durable power of attorney for ease and convenience in managing your financial affairs.

Minor Children

Unfortunately, you cannot designate a guardian for your minor children under a living trust. This is covered in your will and other documents. However, you should still consider someone who is suitable to take care of your children upon your death. Your successor trustee may serve as the trustee of sub-trusts created under the original trust for the benefit of your children.

Distribution of Assets

When you meet with your attorney you will discuss how, when, and for whom your assets will be distributed.

These instructions are pivotal to ensuring your beneficiaries inherit your estate in a way that you dictate. For minor children, it may be worth setting some conditions and milestones that are reflective of your desires for their futures.

In Closing on Living Trusts...

The urgency with which any individual should execute a revocable living trust depends on your stage in life, the nature and amount of your assets, and other circumstances unique to each case. Everyone should discuss a revocable living trust with their attorney.

In California, if your assets are valued under $166,000 (gross), then you may be well served by a will and your power of attorney. It all depends on your future goals.

Again, I would suggest speaking to your attorney to assess your requirements given your individual circumstances.

CHAPTER 7
WAYS TO AVOID PROBATE

There is a common misconception that having a Last Will and Testament will keep your loved ones out of probate court when you pass.

This is not true.

E
xperts agree that probate is something you want to avoid if you can.
I think I have made that point clear throughout this book. However,
we have not covered alternative ways to avoid probate.

What other methods are there to avoid your estate going to probate court? The
good news is that there are multiple avenues available to you and we will
discuss them in detail in this chapter.

A word of caution though: the options discussed below may seem like no-
brainers, but it is always advisable to consult your attorney to discuss the pros
and cons of each prospective choice, since in your individual circumstances
there may be tax implications that could negatively impact your situation.

States differ in how they each administer their own law. There may be
provisions you are unaware of that will derail your plans in a particular state.
Always consult a licensed, qualified lawyer who knows the law in your
jurisdiction.

Payable-On-Death Bank Accounts

Colloquially called the "poor man's trust," payable-on-death bank accounts (or
PODs) are accounts that hold money that can be accessed without the probate
court's involvement.

With these accounts, all you need to do is nominate a beneficiary that will inherit the money in the account or certificate of deposit upon your death, and the bank will do the rest. To claim ownership of the asset following your death, your beneficiary will need to present your bank with a certified copy of your death certificate and proof of their identity. In the event the account was held by joint holders, and both have died, the beneficiary will need death certificates for both.

During your life, the beneficiary cannot access the funds from the POD because they have no legal rights to it. The POD allows you remarkable flexibility to withdraw some or all the funds, change the beneficiary, or close the account all together.

As the account holder, the POD also benefits you by increasing your Federal Deposit Insurance Corporation (FDIC) protection. The standard FDIC coverage limit for an individual's account held at a financial institution is $250,000. However, since a POD is similar in concept to a revocable living trust, the FDIC allows for up to a total of $1,250,000 coverage for five accounts held with a financial institution, where each account has a separate beneficiary assigned.

Instead of depositing $250,000 in each of five different banks to avoid exceeding the $250,000 FDIC coverage limit, you can have multiple PODs in a single bank and still be assured of increased coverage up to five times the standard coverage limit. Check with your bank before depositing sums of money in excess of $250,000 into one account.

The Downsides of a POD Account

Despite its simplicity, flexibility, and cost effectiveness, a POD has its fair share of downsides:

You cannot name alternate beneficiaries with a POD. This means you can only select one person to inherit the funds per POD, and if that nominated individual dies before you, the contents of the POD automatically transfer to an estate or will.

Creditors or disgruntled family members may reach the funds held in the POD. Avoiding probate is one thing, but neglecting debts, child support, or other legal obligations is quite another. Those claims can be asserted against your revocable PODs in court.

Transfer-on-Death Accounts for Securities

Transfer-on-Death Accounts (or TODs) have some similarities to PODs. They entitle designated beneficiaries to receive securities at the time of an individual's death without going through the probate process. Beneficiaries of TODs are also unable to access the securities or other assets while the owner is alive.

Unlike the POD, as the account holder, you can specify how many securities/assets are to be transferred to each beneficiary. You need not name only a single beneficiary. You can distribute securities to multiple beneficiaries and decide how the asset is to be split between them.

If you are unmarried, you can select anyone to be a beneficiary of your brokerage account. However, if you are married, your spouse will legally be entitled to some, or all, of the securities held by you after your death unless they signed a release when the account was created. Importantly, if you and your spouse hold the TOD jointly, upon your death, your spouse will be free to change the beneficiaries. This is a significant feature to remember if you have children from a prior marriage whom your spouse may choose to disinherit.

If the TOD conflicts with your will, the TOD will usually prevail. To avoid any unintended result, you and your attorney should ensure that all your estate planning documents are coordinated so that each is drafted in context with the others.

Initiating a TOD

After your death, when your beneficiaries want to activate your TOD asset, your brokerage firm will require specific documentation to verify the securities are transferred to your beneficiaries in the proportion you decided before death.

The information the brokerage firm may request from your beneficiary includes:

- a death certificate confirming your passing;
- current court letter of appointment (this could mean opening a probate); or
- other documents to prove your death.

The information may vary depending on the account ownership structure, i.e., whether it is jointly held, whether the joint account holders are both deceased, and whether a trust holds the account.

Brokerage firms have been known to be finicky when it comes to recognizing the validity of documents. It is best to check what they deem as the appropriate authority to certify the requested documents and any other information that could help expedite the process for your beneficiaries.

Brokerage firms have been known to be finicky when it comes to recognizing the validity of documents.

Transfer-on-Death Car/Boat Registration

TODs can also extend to cars, boats, and other vehicles. Like other forms of TODs, the assets are transferred to your designated beneficiaries shortly after death and subject to strict documentary requirements. No probate proceedings required.

Not all states allow for TOD registration, but those that do include:

- Arizona
- California
- Connecticut
- Indiana
- Kansas
- Missouri
- Nebraska
- Nevada
- Ohio
- Vermont

Bypassing the Will

Transfer of vehicles registered under a TOD from the deceased to the beneficiary occurs separate and apart from your will. In fact, the vehicle is not considered part of your probate estate and as such does not fall under the jurisdiction of the executor. That means an executor is not required to manage this component of your estate.

While a will and its executor are both important in your overall estate plan, transferring a vehicle under a TOD is a simple exercise not requiring too much intervention.

Claiming a Vehicle

If you are a beneficiary of a vehicle that is titled with a TOD, you need to be aware of the process your state requires to claim the property. Each of the states permitting TOD vehicle registration has its own process to complete vehicle transfers-on-death. It is a good idea to refer to your state's motor vehicle registry authority's website to learn exactly what documents you will need and where to present them.

Typically, most states' requirements to execute a TOD vehicle transfer to a beneficiary are similar, with the basic documents including the following:

- A certificate of title to the vehicle designating you as the beneficiary or one of the beneficiaries; and
- A certified copy of the death certificate.

Locating the title certificate is important. Without it, no transfer will occur until a duplicate title is obtained. While a TOD of your vehicle is usually easily processed, complications may arise.

Multiple Beneficiaries of a Single Vehicle

There may be more than one person named as TOD beneficiaries of a vehicle, which may create a tug-of-war. The car or truck cannot be cut in two, so the beneficiaries will need to resolve the problem through negotiation. Are they each agreeable to sharing ownership and splitting driving time? Do they want to sell it and share the proceeds? Or will one beneficiary buy out the other's interest and take full title?

Impact of Divorce

When a spouse is named as beneficiary with a TOD, a subsequent divorce does not void the designation. Even if you remarry, unless you change the TOD beneficiary, your former spouse will remain the beneficiary. State law will determine the ultimate result, so it is wise to check with your attorney to learn how such issues can be avoided or resolved.

Outstanding Debts

The beneficiary of the TOD will also inherit the debt.

Transfer-on-Death Deeds for Real Estate

The following states offer Transfer-on-Death Deeds:

Alaska	Nebraska
Arizona	Nevada
Arkansas	New Mexico
California	North Dakota
Colorado	Ohio
District of Columbia	Oklahoma
Hawaii	Oregon
Illinois	South Dakota
Indiana	Texas
Kansas	Utah
Maine	Virginia
Minnesota	Washington
Mississippi	West Virginia
Missouri	Wisconsin
Montana	Wyoming

At the time of this writing, the Uniform Real Property Transfer on Death Act was introduced and remains pending in the legislatures of four other states: Connecticut, Rhode Island, Mississippi, and Iowa.

While some states may not currently allow for this precise form of TOD deed, others have similar concepts. For example, Michigan has the similar concept called the Lady Bird Deed.

If your property is not located in a state that recognizes TOD, there are other ways you can avoid having your real estate go through probate proceedings. For example, you can transfer your property to a revocable living trust, as discussed earlier, or consider other asset protection strategies. To learn more about probate avoidance strategies speak with a qualified estate planning attorney in your area.

Ownership

If you are married, the TOD deed will often list you as "joint tenants with rights of survivorship" or "tenants by the entirety." In California, married couples will often take title to the property as "community property with rights of survivorship." It is important to note that the way your property is titled could have significant tax implications. A husband and wife holding title as joint tenants with rights of survivorship are treated differently than a husband and wife who hold as community property with rights of survivorship. Put simply, when a surviving spouse sells real estate that was held jointly, they may be liable for capital gains taxes. Were the same property held as community property with rights of survivorship in a community property state, no capital gains tax would be due in some scenarios.

A transfer on death deed that is held jointly will only transfer upon the last joint owner's passing. No probate court needs to be involved for either the surviving spouse to take title, or for the beneficiary of the joint TOD property to obtain title when the second spouse passes away.

We will discuss the concept of joint tenancy in the next section, as it is a popular option for those looking to sidestep probate. However, like all probate-avoiding options, there are advantages and some drawbacks to be aware of.

Advantages

Like other TOD deeds, the benefits include the following:

- **Avoiding Probate:** A property transferred by a will does not avoid probate, but a TOD deed will.

- **More Affordable than a Living Trust:** If your property portfolio is relatively small, a TOD deed offers protection from probate like a living trust, but for significantly less money. Nevertheless, based on your attorney's assessment, a living trust may be the preferred method. Your property will not avoid probate if the TOD beneficiary predeceases you. A living trust ensures your assets are protected in several unknown, and unforeseen scenarios.

- **Tax Savings:** If your beneficiary decides to sell the property within one year from the date of your death, capital gains will be based on the value of the property at the time of your death as opposed to the acquisition price you paid for the property. This is also true for property that passes through a living trust.

Disadvantages

- **Lost Privacy:** Unlike a will which is filed with the public probate court after death, a TOD deed must be recorded with the land office clerk when the deed is created. That means that your children, and everyone else in town, can find out that you are leaving your property to one child and not another. One of the benefits of avoiding probate is preserving your privacy. A TOD deed fails to do that.

- **Gift Can Lapse:** If one of your beneficiaries predeceases you but is survived by living children those children would have no right to claim any of the property left to their parent in a TOD deed. Most individuals want to ensure their beneficiaries children are cared for in the beneficiary's absence. Using a TOD deed is not suitable for many families.

Joint Tenancy

This is a popular mechanism for avoiding probate. Under this approach, property owned jointly (i.e., under a joint tenancy) automatically passes to the surviving owner(s), without probate. Not only does this transfer happen seamlessly, but the cost is minimal.

Joint tenancy is often an approach used by couples when acquiring property, bank accounts, securities, and other assets. Despite the obvious appeal, there are some significant drawbacks that should concern you.

Here are some of the main disadvantages of a joint tenancy:

- Probate <u>is not</u> avoided completely. Probate is avoided only when the second (or subsequent) joint tenant takes the property following the first joint tenant's death. The transfer of a property between the last owner and the beneficiary will go through probate, unless the last owner wisely used a probate-avoiding method, such as transferring the assets to a Living Trust or using TODs.

- An owner's incapacity may impact other owners. If a joint owner suddenly became incapacitated, this would impact the other joint owners and restrict what they could and could not do. A way to prepare for such a scenario is to have each joint owner sign a "Durable Power of Attorney" authorizing someone to manage their affairs in the event of incapacitation or, you guessed it, transferring the property to a living trust.

While conceptually a joint tenancy may seem like a good idea, you must weigh the benefits and risks and apply these to your personal circumstances.

Tenancy by the Entirety

Like a joint tenancy, this is a popular approach to avoiding probate, but it is reserved exclusively for married couples (and in some states, civil unions, and same-sex partners).

The states that allow for tenancy by the entirety ownership include:

Alaska	Kentucky	Oregon
Arkansas	Maryland	Pennsylvania
Delaware	Massachusetts	Rhode Island
Florida	Michigan	Tennessee
Hawaii	Missouri	Vermont
Illinois	New Jersey	Virginia
Indiana	New York	Washington D.C.
Kentucky	North Carolina	Wyoming
Maryland	Ohio	
Indiana	Oklahoma	

However, some of these states only allow for tenancy by the entirety for specific assets (real estate or homestead properties). Michigan deems the tenancy to exist automatically by virtue of a marriage. In Ohio, only deeds created before April 4, 1985, can be held as tenants by the entirety. Like so many rules in estate planning, laws do differ from state to state. As always, it is necessary to consult with your estate planning attorney to check which assets can be held as tenancy by the entirety in your state.

A major difference between a joint tenancy and a tenancy by the entirety is that a spouse who is a tenant by the entirety cannot transfer his or her share of the property without the other spouse.

Community Property with Right of Survivorship

If you live in one of several community-property states, spouses or registered domestic partners can avoid probate all together by holding title to a piece property as "community property with the right of survivorship."

Right now, there are nine community property states and only six of them permit ownership designated as "community property with right of survivorship. They are Alaska, Arizona, California, Idaho, Nevada, and Wisconsin.

In the states where it is recognized, the legal designation "community property" is a classification that applies to you and your spouse/partner irrespective of how title is held. Most property you or your spouse acquire during the marriage is included under the community property umbrella.

_____ 🌳 _____

Joint tenancy may result in the surviving spouse
to pay capital gains tax on the sale of the property.

The property or assets that are not community property are those that you or your spouse inherited, received as a gift, and any property or income that you and your spouse specifically excluded by agreement in writing. Likewise, you and your spouse/registered partner can agree in writing to specify the assets that should be classified as community property in the same way as a joint tenancy or tenancy by the entirety.

When either spouse/partner dies, the property is transferred to the surviving person without having to go through probate.

One of the major advantages to holding your property as community property is the tax benefit when the first spouse dies. When someone inherits property, an issue to be determined is what value (or basis) will be assigned to the property for tax purposes. In most circumstances, the assigned basis is the value of the property at the time of the owner's death. If the basis was set at a lower price than the current property value, then the beneficiary might need to pay capital gains tax on the difference between the lower price and the value when the property was inherited.

If the property is held as joint tenants, the surviving spouse will only receive a step up in basis on the deceased spouse's ownership interest. However, if the property is held as community property, the surviving spouse will receive a full step up in basis on the property at the death of the first spouse.

Small language differences = large tax impact.

Simplified Probate Proceedings

If you have a 'small' estate, there is some good news. You can avoid probate without having to pursue some of the strategies outlined earlier. With a small estate, you can use what is called a simplified probate process or summary probate.

To the extent you have an estate that does not exceed a certain value, your estate will not have to go through probate following your death. For example, in California the gross value of your estate must be at or below the cap of $166,250 or less (as of January 1, 2022).

If your estate falls under the threshold, your beneficiaries can use the summary probate process. If the estate is of only nominal value, even the summary process may be unnecessary. A lawyer can help your heirs decide which avenue to take.

Calculating Your Estate's Value

The best way to calculate your estate's value is to list all the assets you documented in your will that have designated beneficiaries. Add up the total asset value (gross market value) of your listed items and see whether they exceed or fall under your state's summary probate limit. Do not deduct any outstanding debts on subject property. What you may owe on a mortgage or other debt is not considered in the valuation. The calculation is not on the net value; it is based on the gross value.

Note: Assets held under PODs, TODs, and joint tenancy/equivalent arrangements are excluded from this calculation because they will transfer without going into probate.

If you cannot figure out the value of your assets, you can hire an appraiser to determine the appropriate values. This will result in a more accurate valuation.

The Summary Probate Process

Assuming your estate falls under your state's maximum value cap, your executor or surviving spouse will file a petition in court. The court clerk will usually provide the basic forms. The petition needs to specify your estate's value and what qualifies it for summary probate.

If you have a will, the court will require it to be attached with any documents supporting the petition. If the will does not provide a complete list of your assets, then a separate list or inventory should be attached. This is an unusual occurrence, but it could happen if the will is outdated.

Once the petition has been submitted, the court will allow for a statutory time period for creditors to file a claim against the petitioner. This is where estate vehicles, such as a living trust or other trusts, serve as a shield protecting assets.

If debts or taxes are owed, these will be paid from the estate by the executor before the estate can be distributed to the beneficiaries. While this may appear to a cumbersome process, this process often takes significantly less time than the usual probate process – months as opposed to years.

The Uniform Probate Code (UPC)

Eighteen states[1] have adopted the Uniform Probate Code (UPC) which governs another simplified probate process.

---

[1] National Conference of Commissioners on Uniform State Laws: *Uniform Law Commission*

The UPC provides two different methods for simplified probate, including:

- an affidavit to collect the property, or
- summary administration.

States vary as to whether they allow one or two methods.

Affidavit to Collect the Property

Under this method, beneficiaries of your estate can simply use an affidavit to claim your assets. Your beneficiaries must claim title to your property by signing an affidavit. This method works well for estates that are not subject to legal disputes. If an issue is contested, then the probate court will have to hold a hearing.

Summary Administration

This process functions in much the same way as the summary probate process discussed above. Each state's probate law sets a threshold estate value, and an estate that falls below the threshold can be handled in a less formal, summary process. If your estate falls under the threshold limit, the executor of your will or your spouse can distribute your assets to your designated beneficiaries.

Life Insurance

Generally, life insurance is paid directly to the policy's beneficiary and is not included in the estate. That is why it is rare to have life insurance payouts go through probate. The only two scenarios in which a life insurance policy will end up in probate are if you fail to name a beneficiary on your life insurance policy before your death, or when the named beneficiary predeceased you.

Make sure you nominate a beneficiary on your life insurance policy and your beneficiary will receive the policy amount directly, without any probate issue. The more efficient method is to name a trust as the beneficiary. This method eliminates the worry that a beneficiary may die before you.

When Life Insurance Goes to Probate

If your beneficiary dies before you and you have not updated the policy with an alternative beneficiary to receive the proceeds, the insurance proceeds will have to go through probate. The court will have to decide who should receive the proceeds given the designated beneficiary is not there to receive the funds. The funds will be paid to your estate and will be distributed in accordance with your will (if you have one), less court costs, creditor claims, and attorney fees. If you do not have a will the insurance proceeds will then be distributed to your legal heirs in accordance with your state's law of intestate succession.

The Will vs Insurance Policy

If your will names a beneficiary that differs from the one on your insurance policy, the insurance policy beneficiary will prevail. To accomplish a thorough, integrated estate plan, you need to ensure all beneficiaries named by the will or in any insurance policy are precisely whom you intend to receive the asset. For example, if your wife is listed as the beneficiary of your insurance policy in your will, but you originally designated your brother on the policy many years ago, your brother is legally entitled to receive the insurance proceeds upon your death, not your wife.

One way to ensure your insurance policy has a beneficiary is to name your trust as the beneficiary. You may change your trust throughout your lifetime and would not have to worry about ensuring your life insurance beneficiary is up to date. Naming your trust as a beneficiary ensures your intended heirs will receive the life insurance payout.

One way to ensure your insurance policy has a beneficiary is to name your trust as the beneficiary.

Your Taxable Estate Value

Your life insurance proceeds are not subject to income tax, but they are included in your total estate value for estate tax purposes. That means, that if your estate value is close to the estate tax threshold, your family members are at risk of paying the estate tax. The Tax Reform and Jobs Act of 2017 (TCJA) increased the estate value that is exempt from federal estate tax.

For the tax year 2022, any individual estate valued at less than $12.06 million is exempt from federal estate tax. This number is doubled for married couples. Certain gifts given by the decedent in the years prior to death may be counted against that amount. You should consult with an estate attorney and your tax specialist to address these issues if your estate's value is near that threshold limit. It is important to meet with a qualified estate planning attorney to discuss ways of taking advantage of the current laws before they impact your financial legacy.

The Gift Tax Threshold

Making gifts to beneficiaries is usually a tax-free option that you can exercise without having to go through probate.

As of 2022, you can legally give gifts to your beneficiaries up to a value of $16,000 per person, per year, and not have to pay any gift tax and does not count against your lifetime exemption amount. This limit does not apply to gifts made to a non-citizen spouse.

In the event your gift exceeds $16,000 in cash or assets, you will have to file a gift tax return (i.e., a Form 709), but not necessarily pay any gift tax. The IRS will deduct any amount above the annual exclusion from your lifetime exclusion amount, discussed next.

Example: You and your spouse want to give your daughter $64,000 for a down payment on her first home but you don't want to dip into your lifetime exclusion. You and your spouse can each gift her $16,000 for a total of $32,000. If your daughter is married, you and your spouse may consider giving her spouse an additional $16,000 for the additional $32,000.

Should you decide not to give your daughter's spouse the additional gift, but give it all to your daughter, you would need to file a gift tax return for $32,000.

You would file the gift tax form (IRS Form 706) with your annual income tax return. This form is used to track the value of gifts given over your lifetime and what amount will be deducted from the lifetime exclusion limit.

If you use up the full lifetime exclusion, then your estate can expect to pay a gift tax that ranges between 18% and 40% of the amount that exceeds the exemption. However, this tax rate is subject to change.

Lifetime Exclusion

Currently, the 2022 Lifetime Gift Tax exclusion is $12.06 million. Keep in mind that this $12.06 million is the same $12.06 million as the estate tax exemption. Whatever amount you use throughout your life will be deducted from the lifetime exclusion amount.

Using the example above, if you opt to exclude your daughter's spouse from the $32,000 gift and opt to give the additional $32,000 to your daughter, then IRS Form 706 is filed and the additional $32,000 is subtracted from your $12.06 million.

One thing to keep in mind with the fluctuation of the estate and gift tax exclusion is that it is a use-it-or-lose-it benefit. With the very real possibility of the exclusion amount sunsetting back to $5 million (adjusted for inflation) in 2025, it is advisable for clients to utilize their larger exclusion before the law changes to a lower amount.

CHAPTER 8
RETIREMENT PLANNING

The question isn't at what age I want to retire, it's at what income.

— George Foreman

R etirement plans are popular components of many estate plans. They provide smart tax-saving incentives and could make the difference between retiring well and not being able to retire at all.

In this chapter we'll discuss Individual Retirement Accounts (IRA) as well as 401(k), 403(b), 457(b) plans, and a few other options. Your own personal circumstances and risk tolerance will determine which is best for your life.

This chapter is not intended to replace financial advice from a qualified retirement planner. I recommend meeting with a retirement strategy specialist to discuss your financial blueprint and determine which retirement strategies will help you achieve your goals.

Individual Retirement Accounts

An Individual Retirement Account (IRA) is a form of a <u>qualified</u> retirement plan that serves to increase an individual's retirement savings, while providing significant tax savings.

Each IRA differs in tax treatment, investment strategy, and contribution limits. There are several types of IRAs available today, including traditional IRAs, Roth IRAs, SEP IRAs, and SIMPLE IRAs.

Traditional IRA

Anyone can set up an IRA and hold investments ranging from stocks and bonds to Exchange Traded Funds (ETFs) and mutual funds. The funds deposited will be your own and this is something people often consider if their employer doesn't offer a retirement plan (typically the 401(k) plan) or if they've maxed out their 401(k) employer contributions for that year.

IRAs often enable investors to be masters of their own destiny with investment decisions and afford them access to a wider selection of investments, including private placements, bonds, and real estate. Some individuals defer to financial advisors or other institutions for investing decisions. This may be advisable unless you are familiar with investing and the risks.

Under an IRA, you can contribute up to $6,000 per year if you're under age 50. These contribution limits remain unchanged by the IRS in 2022. If you are 50 and over, you can contribute more to the IRA. It's called a "catch-up" contribution designed to permit those who started saving later in life to progress faster. Those over 50 years old can contribute up to $7,000 per year.

Tax Implications

The contributions you make to your IRA are tax-deductible. However, the extent to which you are entitled to the tax deduction depends on your income and whether you have a retirement plan at work.

A summary of the tax deductions you can expect to receive on your contributions to your IRA are illustrated below.

DEDUCTION LIMITS IF YOU HAVE A RETIREMENT PLAN AT WORK	
2022 Modified Adjusted Gross Income (MAGI)	Deduction
SINGLE OR HEAD OF HOUSEHOLD	
$68,000 or less	Full deduction up to your contribution level
More than $68,000 but less than $78,000	Partial deduction
$78,000 or more	No deduction
MARRIED FILING JOINTLY	
$109,000 or less	Full deduction up to your contribution level
More than $109,000 but less than $129,000	Partial deduction
$129,000 or more	No deduction
MARRIED FILING SEPARATELY	
Less than $10,000	Partial deduction
$10,000 or more	No deduction

While you are entitled to tax deductions on contributions made into your IRA, your withdrawal of this money during retirement will be treated as taxable income and taxed accordingly. The original theory was that retirees would be in a lower tax bracket and would be taxed at a lower rate. This may or may not still hold true, but you certainly should consult a tax lawyer or a certified public accountant before deciding on a plan.

Another feature to keep in mind is the "required minimum distribution" (RMD) that you must take from age 72. Failure to take the required distribution from a traditional IRA may incur a tax penalty of up to 50% of the RMD.

If you withdraw money from your IRA before the age of 59½, you will likely be subject to an early-withdrawal penalty of 10% unless you withdraw $10,000 or less and can demonstrate an extraordinary need fitting one of the IRS hardship criteria.

Roth IRA

Unlike the traditional IRAs, Roth IRA contributions are not tax deferred and are counted as income at the time you contribute the money. The benefit to the Roth IRA is that all the growth on the funds is tax free.

The beauty of the Roth IRA is that while contributions to the Roth IRA are made with after-tax income, the money you generate within the IRA, will never be taxed again. That means all the profits are tax free.

There is no required minimum distribution and no taxes on investment income throughout your retirement.

Unfortunately, Roth IRAs are subject to the same contribution limits as the traditional IRAs. Also, there are limits on how much you can contribute to your Roth IRA, depending on your income.

These limits are set out on the following page.

2022 MAGI	Contribution Limits
SINGLE, HEAD OF HOUSEHOLD, or MARRIED FILING SEPARATELY and you <u>did not</u> <u>live with your spouse</u> at any time during the year	
Less than $129,000	Up to the limit
$129,000 - $144,000	Reduced amount
$144,000 or more	Zero
MARRIED FILING SEPARATELY and <u>you lived with your spouse</u> at any time during the year	
Less than $10,000	Reduced amount
$10,000 or more	Zero
MARRIED FILING SEPARATELY or QUALIFYING WIDOW(ER)	
Less than $204,000	Up to the limit
$204,000 - $214,000	Reduced amount
$214,000 or more	Zero

The tax benefits that the Roth IRA offers during retirement is the primary reason it is often favored over the traditional IRA.

SEP IRA

A Simplified Employee Pension (SEP) IRA is often the choice of taxpayers who are self-employed or freelancers with no employees. Their contributions are fully deductible from their taxable income since they do not have work-based retirement plans.

Like all IRAs, they are subject to annual contribution limits, however, these are significantly higher than other IRAs. For the tax year 2022, the annual contribution limit is the lesser of $61,000 or 25% of annual income.

SIMPLE IRA

The Savings Incentive Match for Employees IRA (SIMPLE) is a retirement plan often provided by small businesses with up to 100 employees.

The plan operates in a similar way to a 401(k) plan, with contributions being made on pre-tax income and the funds being tax-deferred until retirement. Employers are also required to make contributions under a SIMPLE IRA.

The SIMPLE IRA contribution limit is $14,000 as of 2022. However, taxpayers are entitled to an additional $3,000 contribution once they hit age 50, called a catch-up contribution.

Employer Retirement Plans

Your employer may offer a retirement plan, called a 401(k) plan. These plans are popular due to these features:
- tax benefits (i.e., tax is deferred until retirement); and
- employer matching contributions (employer's contribution can match up to 6% of the employee salary).

The contribution limit in 2022 is $20,500 per year until age 50. Those 50 years of age or older can contribute another $6,500, as the catch-up contribution. That means they can contribute up to $27,000 per year to their 401(k) plan.

If you're lucky to have an employer that matches your contributions, they may do so up to 6% of the contribution value. However, if your employer has this policy, check to see whether there is a vesting period before your employer makes the contributions to your 401(k)-plan.

For example, your employer's matching funds may only be fully available if you work for 5 years or longer. If you work less than 5 years you may only be able to access a portion of the funds your employer contributed.

If you work for a non-profit employer, your 401(k) account is called a 403(b); and if you are a government employee, your plan would be called a 457(b).

Tax Implications

Like your IRA, the contributions made to your 401(k) plan will be made pre-tax, lowering your taxable income and the amount of income tax you pay to the IRS, during the year of contributions. Your investment gains will also be tax-free until you withdraw the funds during retirement. If you withdraw funds from your 401(k) before you hit 59 ½, you can be penalized with a 10% penalty.

Disadvantages of 401(k)

While tax deferment and employer-matching funds have increased the appeal of 401(k) plans, they do come with some inherent risks and disadvantages.

Investment choices for these plans are typically limited. Additionally, the management and administrative fees can be costly.

Money held in 401(k) plans are invested in the stock market. The volatility in the market can have an impact on the value of your account plan. The 2008 global financial crisis highlighted the risks of only holding 401(k) accounts for retirement. Unfortunately, some 401(k) accounts lost up to 70% of their value.[1] Many people who were nearing retirement around that time found their dreams delayed or destroyed.

Assets held in 401(k) accounts are not insured by the government. Like any investment, your money may grow, stagnate, or shrink in value over time. Historically these investments have grown, sometimes considerably.

A 401(k) plan is a great way to build your nest egg for retirement. However, it is best used as a wealth builder in conjunction with a diversified investment strategy.

Choosing Beneficiaries for Individual Retirement Programs

When you open any retirement account, you will need to fill out a beneficiary designation form. This form is used to clarify how and to whom you intend to distribute that money upon your death. It is important that you give considerable attention to this form because your beneficiaries named on this designation will override the beneficiaries documented in your will and/or trust.

---

[1] Forbes (2012) *Make Sure You Understand the Benefits and Risks of IRAs and 401(k)s.*

Failure to complete this form will mean that the default arrangements in the custodial agreement will determine how the funds in your retirement accounts are to be distributed. Typically, the funds default to your estate, with all the delay and cost of the probate process.

Naming Your Spouse

It makes sense to choose your spouse as the primary beneficiary, and it's the choice of most people. By designating your spouse as the primary beneficiary, your spouse will have the greatest flexibility when it comes to distribution options.

Your spouse can choose to liquidate a part or all of the account, or they may decide to roll the account into their own IRA account. If your spouse is younger than you, this may be advantageous from a tax perspective because they won't need to worry about withdrawing funds or receiving distributions until a later date.

By designating your spouse as the primary beneficiary, your spouse will have the greatest flexibility when it comes to distribution options.

One downside of naming your spouse is that they may remarry or have children from another relationship. If you have children with your spouse, the likelihood of them providing for your joint children is generally good. However, if your children are from a prior relationship, the situation can become more complicated. You may need additional planning.

When considering naming a beneficiary other than your spouse, pay close attention to property laws of your state. Your spouse may still have a claim against the assets within the account in a community property state even if they are not named as a beneficiary.

Naming a Trust

Naming a trust as your beneficiary limits the flexibility afforded to your spouse but doing so will give you more control over your assets long after you've departed.

Upon your death, the administrator will step in and distribute your assets according to the trust's directions. However, in pursuing this strategy, your trust documentation must be drafted in a specific way to avoid complications. Keep in mind, though, most IRAs hold modest amounts of money. Going through the trust process may be more costly than the account holdings justify. This is a discussion to have with your estate planning attorney.

If you decide to name a trust as the beneficiary to your IRA, or other qualified retirement plan, make sure that you fully understand the tax ramifications of making such an election.

Naming Your Children or Grandchildren

You may decide to name your children or grandchildren as direct beneficiaries of your retirement accounts. If either child is under the legal age, you will have to name a guardian who will manage the funds until the children reach the age of majority.

Naming your children as beneficiaries can present some complications. If your child has special needs and is receiving government assistance, receiving funds from an IRA may disqualify them for assistance.

Some children and young adults need additional time to mature once they turn 18. Entrusting them with a large sum of money can be detrimental to their future. Safeguarding their inheritance over time may be the best option. It is best to discuss these options with your estate planning attorney.

Naming Other Beneficiaries

You are not limited in naming your spouse, children, and grandchildren as your beneficiaries. You may elect to name a good friend or a charity. The choice is yours completely.

CHAPTER 9
TAXES AND YOUR ESTATE

The estate tax punishes years of hard work and robs families of part of their heritage by imposing a huge penalty on inheritance after death – a tax on money that has already been taxed.

— Mike Fitzpatrick

U nderstanding the tax implications of your estate can make a significant difference to your family and how they benefit from your estate. Preplanning can give you an opportunity to reduce, or even eliminate, estate taxes upon your passing. If your estate includes certain types of property you may need to focus on capital gains tax, income tax and property tax.

It is not uncommon to have a client at my conference table looking at me with perplexation when I bring up various tax scenarios. Generally, people do not understand the myriad of ways the government can tax our assets and our estates. I really cannot blame people. For the most part, we are exposed to income tax and sales tax on a regular basis.

This chapter is meant to be a primer for the various ways your estate may be impacted by taxes and how some of the taxes can be avoided. I firmly believe these matters need to be fully discussed with your estate planning attorney, but hopefully with the information contained in this chapter you will be able to keep up with the conversation.

Federal Estate Tax

Oftentimes people refer to the federal estate tax as the "death tax." This tax is imposed on the assets you leave behind when you die. Over the years, Congress has given the people a "break" from this tax, so long as the assets left behind are valued under a certain amount. This threshold value is known as the Federal Estate and Gift Tax Exemption.

To determine the total value of your estate at the time of passing the IRS will consider the following:

- the current market value of your assets on the date of death; and
- any credits and estate tax deductions against the total value of the assets.

Currently, as of 2022, the Estate and Gift Tax Exemption amount is $12.06 million per individual. This number can be doubled for married couples.

The Estate and Gift Tax Exemption amount is set to sunset back to $5 million, adjusted for inflation, in 2025.

If the total assets in your estate are valued under $12.06 million, then **no tax is imposed.** However, if the value exceeds the exclusion amount, the IRS will tax all assets over the exemption amount at the highest tax rate, currently 40 percent.

It is important to note that your estate tax exemption is also reduced by gifts made over the annual exemption throughout your life. For example, if you wanted to give your daughter $50,000 as a down payment on her first home, you would need to claim the $34,000 above the current annual gift exemption of $16,000. To do this, you would have your tax preparer file Form 706 with your annual return claiming the $34,000 as a gift. The IRS will ensure this amount is deducted from your lifetime amount.

If you want to gift your mom a Malibu home worth $13 million, you will exhaust your entire lifetime exemption. You will owe a gift tax calculated on the amount gifted more than the exclusion. Since you exhausted your lifetime estate and gift tax exemption during your lifetime, all your assets will be subject to federal estate tax at the time of your death.

The Unlimited Marital Deduction

The unlimited marital deduction entitles a spouse to transfer assets, irrespective of value, to their spouse and avoid the estate and gift tax. This transfer can be made during life or after death. It is important to note that the unlimited marital deduction is only available for citizen spouses and some non-citizen spouses. It is best to discuss your spouse's citizenship status with your estate planning attorney as the laws may be applied differently.

The marital deduction is a "deflect and defer" tax strategy. Although your estate avoided the gift and estate tax upon your passing by transferring all your assets to your spouse, your spouse's estate may not be as fortunate.

Estate Tax "Portability"

The portability provision effectively allows you to shift any unused federal estate tax exemption over to your spouse at the time of your death. This in turn allows your spouse to use the unused portion at his/her own death and to add it to their individual lifetime estate tax exemption.

If you exercise this option, your executor must document this in the federal estate tax return. The return would indicate that the portability option has been exercised so the IRS is on notice and will have it on record when your spouse dies.

For example, if you die and leave your spouse all your assets, you will avoid using any of your estate and gift tax exemption. Your spouse may then elect to preserve your exemption and stack it on top of theirs. This would allow your spouse to transfer up to double the assets at their passing without paying estate tax.

State Estate and Inheritance Tax

Another type of "death" tax is an inheritance tax which is a tax paid by your beneficiaries on the property they inherit. The good news is that as of 2022 the inheritance tax is only levied by the following six states:

- Iowa
- Kentucky
- Maryland
- Nebraska
- New Jersey
- Pennsylvania

None of the states levy the tax on the decedent's spouse, and only Nebraska and Pennsylvania impose the tax on the decedent's children and grandchildren. The inheritance tax rate is dependent on how close you are to the beneficiary, and in which state the decedent lived. The closer the relationship, the lower the tax. If the decedent lived in one of the 44 states with no inheritance tax (California is one of those states), then an heir will not pay inheritance tax, even if the heir lives in one of the six states listed above.

Twelve states have their own estate taxes. Each one has individual rules, rates, and exemptions. You need to discuss this with your estate planning attorney if you live in a state that imposes an estate tax.

Capital Gains Taxes

The capital gains tax is a tax on the difference between the cost basis of the investment and its sale price. In other contexts, cost basis is typically the price paid for the asset. In the context of estates, the cost basis of the assets inherited from a decedent is the market value of the asset on the day the deceased passed away. This is called a "stepped-up basis" and can significantly reduce your beneficiary's tax bill.

If your beneficiary sells an inherited asset over and above its stepped-up basis, then they will likely pay capital gains tax. Conversely, if they sell the asset for less than its stepped-up basis, they will be entitled to recognize a capital loss, which can be deducted against their ordinary income.

Reducing Federal Estate Taxes

Avoiding federal estate taxes is a top priority for many people. As mentioned previously, federal estate tax is the federal tax on your estate's assets over $12.06 million in 2022. This exemption amount is set to be reduced in the year 2025.

There are several strategies that can be used to reduce your estate tax liability. Since everyone's situation is different, it is best to contact an estate planning attorney that focuses on estate tax reduction strategies. It is very important that you contact a qualified tax advisor prior to making any lifetime gifts of property or other appreciated assets. If you proceed with making a transfer without contacting a qualified tax advisor, you could trigger unintended taxable events that could be very costly.

There are several strategies that can be used to
Reduce your estate tax liability.

One strategy to reduce the estate tax burden is by making annual gifts to your loved ones maximizing the annual gift tax exclusion.

The annual gift tax exclusion is a great way to stretch out generational gifts throughout your lifetime without having to report it to the IRS. For the taxable year 2022, the annual gift tax exclusion is $16,000 per person per year. This means that a husband and wife could gift up to $32,000 ($16,000 per spouse) to their child without having to file a gift tax return (IRS Form 709).

For Example, say your daughter is getting married and you want to give her and her spouse money for a down payment on a starter home. You want to give her $64,000 but don't want to report this gift to the IRS. If you are married, you and your spouse would each give $16,000 to your daughter and her spouse.

> Mom gives daughter $16,000
> Dad gives daughter $16,000
> Mom gives daughter's spouse $16,000
> Dad gives daughter's spouse $16,000

Mom and Dad just passed $64,000 to their daughter and her spouse without exceeding the annual exclusion and triggering the need to file a gift tax return.

It is important to keep in mind that the above example does have community property implications that should be discussed with your attorney prior to executing.

To read more about the annual gift tax exclusion, refer to Chapter 7.

Disclaimer Trust Planning

A disclaimer trust is a situational estate planning tool that can provide married couples with flexibility both before and after the passing of a spouse. A disclaimer trust involves the use of an irrevocable trust that is only funded under specific circumstances. Specifically, these trusts are funded when the surviving spouse refuses to accept — or "disclaims" — the distribution of assets from the trust.

Disclaimer trusts are complex planning tools, but they can be advantageous for some married couples considering their options. This approach can have benefits related to income tax liability as well as a host of other factors. Talk to an attorney before you move forward with disclaimer trust planning.

What Is Disclaimer Trust Planning?

Disclaimer trust planning involves one spouse disclaiming assets that they are entitled to inherit from their deceased spouse. This is not an all-or-nothing decision, meaning you could disclaim some assets but not others. Assets that are disclaimed go into a separate trust that is not considered part of the surviving spouse's estate. This is an important distinction, as these assets could pass on to beneficiaries without causing them inheritance tax issues.

When the first spouse dies, the surviving spouse has the option to disclaim some or all of the assets in the disclaimer trust. Any assets that are disclaimed remain in the trust and do not become part of the surviving spouse's estate. The determination of whether marital assets will remain in the surviving spouse's estate or outside of the estate is known as a Clayton Election.

One of the most important aspects of these trusts is that the surviving spouse can still enjoy the proceeds of the trust during their lifetime, even if they disclaim these assets. This estate planning tool gives couples a way to provide for each other after the first spouse's death without causing unwanted tax consequences for future beneficiaries. These are also useful in protecting assets as they appreciate in value.

Disclaimer Trusts Are Optional

One of the most important aspects of a disclaimer trust is that the choice to disclaim the proceeds of the trust is optional. Unlike a credit shelter trust, the surviving spouse has significant flexibility after the passing of their husband or wife. This reduces the potential for a situation where the surviving spouse is forced to disclaim some of the estate assets when it is no longer in their best interest.

Circumstances change, especially when such trusts go into effect many years after they were created. This added flexibility makes disclaimer trusts a powerful estate planning option for many people.

Time Limits and Process

There is an important deadline to understand when it comes to disclaiming trust assets. The beneficiary must disclaim any assets within nine months of the decedent's passing. Once the nine-month period has elapsed, there is no opportunity to disclaim any assets. This means that any assets not disclaimed during that time transfer automatically to the beneficiary.

There are other requirements in addition to this time limit. Not only must any disclaimer be made within the nine-month window but also it must be made in writing. What's more, the disclaimer must be made by the beneficiary. The only exception is if the beneficiary has a conservator. In that case, a conservator has the power to disclaim trust assets on the beneficiary's behalf. The disclaimer must also be filed with the court. This filing must occur within a "reasonable time." While that term is subjective, state law finds that any disclaimer filed within nine months of the decedent's passing is considered reasonable. The courts will consider filings made after the nine months have elapsed on a case-by-case basis.

Leave the Details to Experienced Legal Counsel

Even a minor clerical error could upend the purpose of a disclaimer trust and eliminate the planning objective. Given what is at stake, it is vital to allow an experienced attorney to assist you through every step of the trust creation process.

CHAPTER 10
ATTORNEYS

If you fail to plan, you may as well plan to fail.

— *Benjamin Franklin*

In today's digital age, finding the answer to virtually any problem is as easy as a few clicks of a keyboard. There are a lot of online resources available that offer guidance on a wide range of legal matters, but it is not advisable to rely on generic, online legal guidance for your individual situation. Estate planning is one area of law that has a lot of little nuances that need to be considered to avoid unintended tax penalties.

Online websites like LegalZoom or RocketLawyer make a DIY estate plan appealing with the low cost and easy to navigate platform. The problem with these websites is the "one size fits all" approach. The documents that are produced are not customized, are not drafted by attorneys, and could result in expensive consequences.

Online Guidance Provided is Never Specific to You

While sometimes useful, online guidance is kept intentionally broad because it is intended for readers with very different needs and issues. The articles you read can only offer basic information. Online writers can't possibly understand everyone's specific circumstances.

Engaging an Attorney Saves You Time and Money

One mistake you make with respect to your estate plan can cost you a significant amount of money in unanticipated taxes and legal fees. Over the years, small errors or even a misplaced comma have created enough confusion to send estates into probate courts that would never have been necessary if the documents were drafted more carefully. The delay and expense caused by a carelessly drafted will or trust can be ruinous to your estate.

Attorneys Plan for the Worst-Case Scenario

Your attorney has seen it all. They've been there, done that. They live and breathe law. What your lawyer hears about your life, your assets, and your future plans will be translated into the documents necessary to see that your needs and wishes are provided for the way you intended. Lawyers are trained to look for possible problems and to incorporate solutions before the problems arise.

They will ensure your estate planning covers all the bases. From avoiding probate to preventing legal disputes over your estate, and managing beneficiaries who are minors, your attorney can anticipate the unexpected scenarios that may creep up.

Who Should You Hire?

Two of the most important decisions you can make in your life are whom you hire as your attorney and your accountant. As explained in the previous section, an effective attorney can make the difference between preserving your estate for your children and surrendering your estate decisions to a probate judge, or the IRS.

When looking to engage the right estate attorney, you should consider the following factors:

Where is the attorney located? As you saw in earlier chapters, estate planning laws can vary from state to state. So, it is always best to deal with an estate attorney that is licensed and experienced in your state.

How varied are your assets? Do you have diversified assets in your estate? Do you own interests in one or more businesses? Do you own shares of stocks? Do you hold any bonds? Are you in debt? Are you in a second or subsequent marriage? Do you have children?

How much does the attorney charge? Hopefully, the attorney fee will not become a determining factor in your choice of lawyers. But when shopping for the best lawyer for you, be sure to compare apples to apples. *You cannot compare the cost of a skilled estate lawyer with the fee schedule of a general practitioner who does little estate work.*

Check the lawyer's reputation in the community. Is the lawyer a member of any trust and estate law professional organizations? Has the lawyer received any awards or recognition for excellence related to their trusts and estates practice?

You may not need the lawyer who wrote the book on trusts, but you need to avoid the lawyer who has barely read the book. Find the expert in your comfort zone. You will never regret taking the time to find the best lawyer for you.

<u>What is the office's client engagement process?</u> Typically, you will not always be dealing with one attorney for every interaction you have with the office. Occasionally the attorney's team will get involved in administrative matters, like fielding questions from you, billing, and scheduling. The office will likely have junior lawyers, paralegals, and other staff members performing tasks for which the expertise of the primary lawyer is not necessary.

Working with Your Attorney

Provide as much detail as possible. Providing your lawyer with detail about your circumstances supplies them with the raw material they need to choose clauses, exceptions, and tactics to draft a customized estate plan just for you.

If your attorney is charging by the hour, you do not want repeated phone calls and meetings to fill in data you could simply have provided up front. In fact, I suggest you ask your attorney what information they need before you have your first paid consultation.

Return for an Estate Plan Tune-up Whenever Something Changes

If circumstances in your life change (e.g., you're divorced, widowed, remarried, or you engage in a new business), consult with your attorney early. This affords your attorney the opportunity to revise any relevant estate planning documentation when you are able and available. Waiting creates a risk that your documents will become stale and out of sync with your new situation.

Consider scheduling an annual meeting with your attorney to discuss any changes to your life and whether they impact your estate plan at all. You can always reschedule if nothing relevant has occurred.

Choosing the right lawyer is one of the most
Important decisions you will make.

When you hire an attorney you like, you will probably be working together for years to come. Cooperating successfully means respecting each other's time and competing obligations. Your relationship with your lawyer will thrive if you discuss these topics during your first meeting:

- billing cycles (monthly, quarterly, on-demand)
- best time of day to discuss matters
- preferred mode of communication (in-person, telephone, email)
- level of detail required on new matters (new retainer for each job, repeated terms, etc.)

The attorney-client relationship is ideally one in which both parties know and trust each other. You will need to trust your lawyer and be able to openly discuss private and personal information, including finances and intimate family dynamics. As I said earlier, choosing the right lawyer is one of the most important decisions you will make.

Estate planning is a very detailed area of law that touches each one of us during our lifetime in a different way. We all need an estate plan, but so often people avoid the daunting process. I cannot blame anyone for putting off their planning as the conversation is never easy to have; however, I do strongly encourage everyone to start the process. Even If you think you don't have anything, I assure you that you have something for which to plan.

Your estate plan is one of the greatest gifts you can give your loved ones. When you take the time to make the hard decisions and put a plan in place it allows for your loved ones to grieve peacefully and not have to worry about when to file in probate court.

While I hoped this book would be the definitive layman's resource on estate planning, I need to stress that I am unaware of your personal circumstances. I truly hope you learned a lot from reading these chapters, but if you've gained only one valuable insight, let it be that you need to consult and work with a qualified, experienced estate lawyer to ensure your individual circumstances are the focus of your estate plan.

My law practice, San Diego Legacy Law, PC, assists individuals like you every day and we do so with your interests as our chief focus. Satisfying your requirements is what we live for, and we've been recognized consistently for our superior service.

Should you wish to discuss any aspect of your estate plan, I am only a phone call, email, or visit away. I would be honored to hear from you.

Finally, know that I wish you the best in your estate planning journey, and I trust that this book has provided you enough information to kickstart the process.

Sincerely,

Nicole D'Ambrogi, Esq., LL.M.
Principal
(619) 550-3080
San Diego Legacy Law, PC
www.SDLegacyLaw.com

N icole D'Ambrogi is a distinguished estate planning attorney based in San Diego. Recognized as a Super Lawyers Rising Star, she has built a name for herself in estate planning and probate law and has garnered a reputation as a staunch advocate for veterans. A former member of the U.S. Navy, her practice focuses on comprehensive estate planning and asset protection services. Among numerous other honors, Nicole received the *Women Resiliency Award by the U.S. Department of Veteran Affairs in 2015* and the *Trailblazer Award from the California Department of Veteran Affairs in 2016.*

Nicole developed an interest in becoming a lawyer at a young age and stuck with her dream throughout her Navy service until she entered law school. Looking back, she recalls the journey:

> *"I grew up wanting to be a lawyer. I made all the kids in the neighborhood play court, and I was always the judge. I had it in my*

mind at a young age, and I just never let go of the idea. I went into the Navy telling everybody that I was going to go to law school afterward. I would sit in my barracks room on Friday nights and do homework instead of going out with friends. I wanted to go to law school, and I would only get there with hard work and dedication."

Nicole worked toward her bachelor's degree in management during her time in the Navy. Once she completed her service and graduated from the University of Phoenix in 2010, she headed straight to Thomas Jefferson School of Law in San Diego. While in law school, she volunteered at the Veterans Legal Assistance Clinic and was an integral part of the foundation of the Veterans Self-Help Legal Clinic, which provides pro bono legal services for low-income veterans in San Diego County.

Nicole founded her practice in May 2014 and has since developed a specialty in comprehensive estate planning strategies. Inspired by the mishandling of her grandmother's estate, she is passionate about assisting clients in planning for long-term care and protecting their assets.

As an advocate for veterans, she has worked, notably, with populations of incarcerated female veterans, who often do not have a trustworthy advocate to help them navigate the penal system, and who Nicole takes pride in supporting as they build new lives.

Today, San Diego Legacy Law serves clients throughout San Diego, La Jolla, Del Mar, Carlsbad, Rancho Santa Fe, Oceanside, Poway, Escondido, San Marcos, Fallbrook, and the surrounding areas.

After a successful start to her career, Nicole went back to school to earn her Master of Law in International Taxation, Wealth Management, and Financial Services. This allowed her to expand her practice to include fundamental estate planning, minor children, elder law, veterans' benefits, estate tax planning, probate & estate administration, business succession, asset protection, charitable planning, Medi-Cal crisis planning, special needs planning, civil litigation planning, and civil rights defense.

Outside of serving her wealth management clients, Nicole prioritizes community involvement through local charitable organizations and veteran associations. She is an adjunct professor at Thomas Jefferson School of Law and supervising attorney for the Thomas Jefferson School of Law Veterans Legal Assistance Clinic. She also frequently posts to her blog, where she shares her expertise in the field and sheds light on current trends.

Moving ahead, Nicole looks forward to continuing her work in estate planning and veterans' benefits, providing clients with the highest quality legal representation possible. She is driven by her ability to improve the quality of her clients' lives.

Education & Certifications

- LL.M, International Taxation, Financial Services, and Wealth Management, Magna Cum Laude (2016) – Thomas Jefferson School of Law
- Juris Doctor (2013) – Thomas Jefferson School of Law
- Bachelor of Science in Management (2010) – University of Phoenix
- FINRA Series 7 and NASAA Series 66 Life and Health Insurance License, California Department of Insurance

- Chartered Trust and Estate Planner (CTEP)
- Chartered Wealth Manager (CWM) – GAFM Global Academy of Finance & Management, International Board of Standards
- California State Bar #295028

Awards & Honors

- Rising Star, Super Lawyers (2016-2021)
- Chartered Trust and Estate Planner, GAFM
- Chartered Wealth Manager, GAFM
- Women Resiliency Award, U.S. Department of Veteran Affairs (2015)
- Trailblazer Award, California Department of Veteran Affairs (2016)
- President Pro Bono Service Award, California State Bar (2015)
- San Diego Military Hero Award, Channel 10 and Coleman University (2014)
- Powerhouse Patriot Award (2014)
- VIP Women of the Year, National Association of Professional Women
- Who's Who Among Students in American Universities and Colleges (2013)
- Veterans Clinic Alumni Scholarship (2012)
- Superb 10.0 Avvo Rating, Top Attorney in Estate Planning
- Veteran of the Year, American Combat Veterans of War (2014)

Professional Memberships & Community Involvement

- The Women Veterans Engaging the Nation (WoVEN)
- The American History Theater
- Integrated Recovery Foundation

- San Diego SCRA Pro Bono
- ScholarVet
- Consumer Attorneys of San Diego
- American Combat Veteran of War
- Veterans Bar Association
- San Diego Bar Association
- Phi Alpha Delta
- WAVES
- State Bar of California
- National Association of Professional Women

THE IDEAL SPEAKER FOR YOUR NEXT EVENT

Nicole is a well-articulated speaker who can break down complex legal concepts into ideas anyone can relate to and understand. Her unique communication style creates a relaxed environment that makes it easy for her audience to engage in thought regarding end-of-life planning. Her insights into what can, and will, happen when a plan is not properly in place will inspire your group to move forward with action!

In addition to Nicole's technical knowledge presentations, she is a vibrant motivational speaker on pathways to success and breaking through barriers of fear. She guides her audience through the most common types of fears that hold people back from pursuing their dreams and provides insight on how to push through those fears for personal growth and development. Her motivational keynotes will inspire your audience to conquer all the negative self-doubts that can come up when pushing towards a personal goal.

Nicole's keynote presentations are perfect for corporations, non-profits, conferences, seminars, associations, entrepreneur groups, and fundraising events. Her unique wisdom will leave audiences with the knowledge they need to take action on their dreams and/or their family estate planning.

To invite Nicole to speak at an event, please call (619) 550-3080
Or email nicole@sdlegacylaw.com

CITATIONS

2021 Wills and Estate Planning Study. Caring.com. (n.d.). Retrieved February 4, 2022, from https://www.caring.com/caregivers/estate-planning/wills-survey/

2021-2022 Bill 3821: SC Uniform Transfers to Minors Act - South Carolina Legislature Online. (n.d.). Retrieved February 4, 2022, from https://www.scstatehouse.gov/sess124_2021-2022/bills/3821.htm

2022 IRA contribution and deduction limits effect of modified AGI on deductible contributions if you are covered by a retirement plan at work. Internal Revenue Service. (n.d.). Retrieved February 4, 2022, from https://www.irs.gov/retirement-plans/plan-participant-employee/2022-ira-contribution-and-deduction-limits-effect-of-modified-agi-on-deductible-contributions-if-you-are-covered-by-a-retirement-plan-at-work

Centers for Disease Control and Prevention. (2020, September 16). *Disability impacts all of us infographic*. Centers for Disease Control and Prevention. Retrieved July 2020, from https://www.cdc.gov/ncbddd/disabilityandhealth/infographic-disability-impacts-all.html/

H.R.1 - 115th Congress (2017-2018): An Act to provide for ... (n.d.). Retrieved July 2020, from https://www.congress.gov/bill/115th-congress/house-bill/1

IRS announces changes to retirement plans for 2022. Internal Revenue Service. (n.d.). Retrieved February 4, 2022, from https://www.irs.gov/newsroom/irs-announces-changes-to-retirement-plans-for-2022

Krooks, B. A. (2012, October 22). *Make sure you understand the benefits and risks of IRAS and 401(k)s*. Forbes. Retrieved July 2020, from https://www.forbes.com/sites/bernardkrooks/2012/10/22/make-

sure-you-understand-the-benefits-and-risks-of-iras-and-
401ks/#169dc5444182/

Mary Randolph, J. D. (2016, January 25). *States that allow transfer-
on-death deeds for real estate.* www.nolo.com. Retrieved
February 4, 2022, from https://www.nolo.com/legal-
encyclopedia/free-books/avoid-probate-book/chapter5-1.html

Probate code. Probate Code - Uniform Law Commission. (n.d.).
Retrieved July 2020, from
https://www.uniformlaws.org/committees/community-
home?CommunityKey=a539920d-c477-44b8-84fe-
b0d7b1a4cca8%2F

*Senate Bill 1305 - An act to amend Section 5600 of the Probate Code,
relating to revocable transfer on death deeds.* Bill Text - SB-
1305 Revocable transfer on death deeds. (n.d.). Retrieved July
2020, from
https://leginfo.legislature.ca.gov/faces/billTextClient.xhtml?bill_
id=201920200SB1305&search_keywords=transfer%2Bon%2Bd
eath%2F

State-by-state guide to inheritance taxes in 2022. Policygenius. (n.d.).
Retrieved February 4, 2022, from
https://www.policygenius.com/estate-planning/state-by-state-
guide-to-inheritance-
taxes/#:~:text=There%20is%20no%20federal%20inheritance,%2
C%20New%20Jersey%2C%20and%20Pennsylvania.

Transfers to Minors Act. Transfers to Minors Act - Uniform Law
Commission. (n.d.). Retrieved July 2020, from
https://www.uniformlaws.org/committees/community-
home?CommunityKey=4b0fd839-f40d-4021-af03-
406e499ca67c%2F